TOTAL
RE
CREATION

VERY IMPORTANT!

I would love to stay in contact with you as we both grow. Please take a picture holding your book and tag me on social media and I will reshare it on my page.

Tag me on Instagram at @officialandyelliott
Or tag me on Facebook and LinkedIn at Andy Elliott

Also, please text me if you need anything at all!
ANDY ELLIOTT (918) 210-0254

TOTAL RECREATION
BY ANDY ELLIOTT

Published by Andy Elliott and The Elliott Group
11010 N. Saguaro Blvd. #100 Fountain Hills, AZ 85268

Printed in the United States of America

Cover and Layout Design by
Brandon Wood @ Woodbird Studio LLC

TOTAL RE CREATION

ANDY ELLIOTT

TABLE OF CONTENTS

THE DAY YOUR LIFE CHANGES FOREVER

This isn't just another self-help book you'll read, feel good about for a few days, then toss on the shelf to gather dust. This is a declaration of war. A war against mediocrity, against the limitations you've placed on yourself, against the voice in your head that whispers, "You're not good enough," or "You'll never amount to anything." This is a battle cry for Total Recreation—a complete and utter annihilation of the old you, the one who settles, the one who's afraid, the one who's been playing small for far too long.

What if I told you that today could be the day everything changes? The day you finally break free from the complacency and limiting beliefs holding you back? The day you ignite your inner fire and start living on your terms?

Whether you feel stuck in a rut, hungry for more success, or know you're meant for something greater, you're in the right place. Because this book isn't just another manual to make you feel good temporarily. It's a wake-up call—your personal invitation to a Total Recreation of your life, a transformation guided by the **WARRIOR Framework**.

Right now, you're standing at a crossroads. You can choose to keep doing what you've always done, accepting the same old results and frustrations and staring back in the mirror. Or you can choose to step onto a path less traveled, a path that leads to a life beyond your wildest dreams. A life of purpose, passion, abundance, and impact. A life where you wake up every morning excited to conquer the day, go to bed at night knowing you left it all on the field, and look in the mirror with pride, recognizing the badass warrior you've become.

I'm Andy Elliott, and alongside my battle mate, my ride-or-die wife, Jacqueline, we've walked this path ourselves. We know firsthand how it feels to be shackled by an "average" existence. For years, we settled for far less than we could, letting our pasts and self-doubts define us. But there came a point when we decided to kill those old versions of ourselves, to shatter our limits and start playing life big. That decision led us on a journey from sleeping on mattresses to building a multi-million dollar business, from struggling in our relationship to becoming a power couple, from living in our little bubbles to becoming leaders making a real impact. And now, we want to show you the exact roadmap we followed, the **WARRIOR Framework**, so you can engineer your own extraordinary transformation.

This book is your guide, battle plan, and blueprint for Total Recreation. It's a journey of transformation, a process of shedding the skin of your past and stepping into the most powerful, authentic version of yourself. It's about breaking free from the bloodlines that have held you back, the generational curses that have whispered limitations in your ear, and the self-sabotaging patterns that have kept you playing small.

Imagine this: You wake up before sunrise, feeling energized and ready to attack the day. Your mind is sharp, body is strong, and spirit is on fire. You hit the gym, pushing your physical limits, knowing that **Workout** is the foundation of a **WARRIOR'S** strength. Jacqueline's right there with me, pushing just as hard because we're united against mediocrity. You dominate your business, crushing your goals, inspiring your team, and making a real impact on the world. You're a leader, a force to be reckoned with, and your success is a testament to the power of hard work, dedication, and unwavering belief in yourself. You understand the importance of **Relationships** and have built an unrecruitable tribe of loyal brothers and sisters who have your back no matter what.

Your relationships are thriving. You have a deep, passionate connection with your spouse, your kids look up to you as their hero, and you're surrounded by a team who have your back no matter what. You've mastered the art of **Integration**, seamlessly blending your work and personal life into a powerful, fulfilling whole. You look in the mirror and see a reflection that makes you proud—a person who's physically fit, mentally strong, and spiritually aligned. You're living a life of purpose, passion, and abundance and inspiring others to do the same. You take **Ownership** of your choices, actions, and impact on the world, knowing that true success comes from within.

This life awaits you on the other side of Total Recreation. It's not a fantasy; it's a reality you can create, one brick at a time, one decision at a time, one day at a time. And the **WARRIOR Framework** is the key to unlocking that reality.

In this book, you'll learn how to:

KILL THE OLD YOU

We'll explore the mindset shifts, habits, and beliefs holding you back and give you the no-BS truth about breaking free from mediocrity. You'll learn to **Recreate** yourself, shedding the skin of your past and embracing the warrior within.

BREAK THE BLOODLINE

You'll learn to identify and overcome the generational patterns and limitations passed down in your family, rewriting your story and creating a new legacy for yourself and your loved ones. You'll develop the **Awareness** to recognize these patterns and the courage to break free.

EMBRACE SACRIFICE

You'll discover why sacrifice is essential for growth and how to make strategic sacrifices that align with your values and propel you toward your goals. You'll understand that true **Ownership** means making tough choices and being willing to pay the price for greatness.

MASTER WORK-LIFE INTEGRATION

You'll learn to create a life where your work and personal life are in harmony, where you're crushing it in business and being the best partner, parent, and friend you can be. You'll master the art of **Integration**, blending your passions and priorities into a powerful, fulfilling whole.

DEVELOP UNWAVERING FOCUS

You'll master the art of "not blinking," cultivating the laser focus and determination that will allow you to power through any obstacle and achieve anything you set your mind to. You'll learn to take **Ownership** of your thoughts and actions, directing your energy towards your goals with unwavering precision.

HARNESS THE COMPOUND EFFECT

You'll understand the power of small, consistent actions over time and how to create daily routines that compound into massive success. You'll embrace the **Workout** pillar, knowing that consistent effort, both physically and mentally, is the key to unlocking your full potential.

BECOME A LEADER

You'll learn to ignite the leader within yourself and inspire others to step into their greatness, building a team of unstoppable forces committed to growth and impact. You'll understand that true leadership builds relationships and empowers others to become leaders.

BUILD A BROTHERHOOD

You'll discover the power of surrounding yourself with a loyal inner circle, a tribe of brothers and sisters who will support you, challenge you, and celebrate your victories. You'll learn to cultivate **Relationships** built on trust, loyalty, and a shared commitment to growth.

DOMINATE IN SALES

You'll master the mindset, strategies, and tactics that will turn you into a sales powerhouse, crushing your goals and building a life of abundance. You'll embrace the **Workout** pillar, knowing that physical and mental strength are essential for success in sales. You'll develop the **Awareness** to understand your customers' needs and the **Ownership** to take responsibility for your results.

NURTURE RELATIONSHIPS

You'll learn to build and maintain strong relationships with the people who matter most, creating a network that fuels your success and enriches your life. You'll master the art of **Relationships**, building a tribe of loyal supporters, advisors, and collaborators.

LIVE A RICH-ASS LIFE

You'll define what a truly fulfilling life looks like and create a plan to make that vision a reality, embracing abundance, purpose, and a lasting legacy. You'll understand that a "rich-ass life" is about **Integration**, aligning all areas of your life with your values and goals. It's about using your success to **Reach** others and positively impact the world.

This is not a journey for the faint of heart. It will require courage, discipline, and a willingness to push past your limits. But I promise you, the rewards are worth every ounce of effort. On the other side of this journey is a life beyond your wildest dreams, a life that makes you proud and leaves a lasting impact on the world.

So, are you ready to kill the old you and step into your power? Are you ready to embrace Total Recreation's challenge, discomfort, and growth? Are you ready to become a **WARRIOR**?

If so, turn the page. Your life will never be the same. Your journey begins now.

THE WARRIOR FRAMEWORK

YOUR BLUEPRINT FOR TOTAL *RECREATION*

You've made the decision to change. You've heard the call to rise above mediocrity and create a life of purpose, passion, and impact. You're ready to wage war against the limitations that have held you back and unleash the unstoppable force within. But every warrior needs a battle plan, a roadmap to victory. That's where the **WARRIOR Framework** comes in.

This chapter is your arsenal, your strategic guide to achieving Total Recreation. It's the blueprint for transforming your body, mastering your mind, building an unbreakable support network, and ultimately becoming the **WARRIOR** you were born to be.

WARRIOR is more than just an acronym; it's a way of life. It's a set of principles that will guide you on a transformation journey, leading you to an unstoppable mindset and a rich-ass life, just like the one I've built with The Elliott Group. It's about breaking the bloodline of mediocrity and becoming the best version of yourself.

THE WARRIOR PILLARS

W *WORKOUT*
Activate your body and mind for war.

A *AWARENESS*
Know yourself - your strengths, weaknesses, and patterns.

R *RELATIONSHIPS*
Build an unrecruitable tribe.

R *RECREATE*
Kill the old you, unleash the **WARRIOR** within.

I *INTEGRATION*
Work-life Integration, not balance.

O *OWNERSHIP*
100% responsibility, zero excuses.

R *REACH*
Impact, influence, and leave a legacy.

The Analogy I Love: Imagine a **WARRIOR** preparing for battle. They train their body and mind (**Workout**), study the terrain and their enemy (**Awareness**), assemble a loyal, unrecruitable army (**Relationships**), forge new armor and weapons (**Recreate**), strategize for a holistic victory (**Integration**), take command of the battlefield (**Ownership**), and fight for a cause greater than themselves (**Reach**).

BREAKDOWN OF EACH PILLAR

1. WORKOUT

- Think of it like this: A warrior doesn't go into battle flabby and out of shape. They train their asses off to build strength, endurance, and resilience. That's what **Workout** is all about. It's not just about looking good but building a **WARRIOR** mindset.

- Let me tell you a story: Remember when Jacqueline called me out on getting "comfortable"? Man, that was a wake-up call! I knew I had to activate my inner warrior. I hit the gym and shaved my head—I was ready to fight for the life I deserved. And that physical transformation fueled my mental transformation.

- Here's the deal:
  - **Invest one hour a day - that's just 4% of your time - to activate your body.** Hit the gym, go for a run, and do whatever gets your blood pumping. This isn't optional; it's non-negotiable.
  - **Treat your body like a Ferrari, not a beat-up clunker.** Fuel it with high-quality food, not junk. You wouldn't put cheap gas in a Ferrari, would you?
  - **There should be no distractions when you're training.** This is your time to focus on yourself. Put your phone on "Do Not Disturb" and get in the zone. This is about building mental toughness, not checking Instagram.

- Here's what you get:
  - **You'll tap into a biological superpower.** Intense workouts release all those feel-good chemicals—dopamine, oxytocin, and serotonin. You'll feel amazing and ready to conquer the day.
  - **Energy and focus through the roof.** You'll be sharper, more alert, and ready to dominate every area of your life.
  - **Confidence that radiates outwards.** You'll feel better about yourself, and it will show.
  - **Resilience like you've never experienced.** You'll be able to handle whatever life throws at you, no sweat.

2. AWARENESS

- **This is about knowing yourself.** A warrior studies the battlefield, understands their enemy, and knows their strengths and weaknesses. They're constantly evaluating themselves and looking for ways to improve. That's the power of Awareness.

- I'll be the first to admit that I didn't shy away from my past, from the bloodline of struggle and limitation. I faced those demons head-on, acknowledged my weaknesses, and sought out mentors like Andy Frisella to guide me. That's **WARRIOR**-level self-awareness.

- Here's how to level up your Awareness:
  - **Ask yourself the tough questions.** What are your weaknesses? What are you afraid of? What are you avoiding? Be brutally honest with yourself, even if it hurts.
  - **Get feedback from your tribe.** Ask your spouse, your team, and your mentors for their honest opinions. Don't be afraid of criticism; use it to improve.
  - **Identify those limiting beliefs.** What are the lies you're telling yourself? Challenge them and replace them with empowering truths.

- The payoff is huge:

  - **Crystal-clear purpose and direction.** You'll know what you want and how to get it. No more wandering around in the dark.

  - **Decision-making is on point.** You'll be able to make better choices and handle challenges like a boss.

  - **Emotional intelligence that's off the charts.** You'll be able to manage your emotions and stay focused on your goals, even when shit hits the fan.

3. RELATIONSHIPS

- Listen up: A warrior doesn't fight alone. They assemble a loyal, unrecruitable army, a band of brothers who fight alongside them and have their back. That's what Relationships are all about. It's about building a tribe of badasses who are more than just colleagues; they're family.

- I've seen this firsthand. From the early days in that tiny office, building my empire brick by brick, to the unwavering support of Jacqueline and my inner circle, I've embodied the power of brotherhood. I know that true strength lies in unity.

- Here's how to build your unrecruitable tribe:

  - **Be intentional about who you surround yourself with.** Choose people who believe in you, support you, and challenge you to improve.

  - **Invest in those relationships.** Spend time with your loved ones, nurture friendships, and build a strong support network.

  - **Create a culture of loyalty.** Treat your team like family, pay them well, and inspire them to be their best. Make them feel like they're part of something bigger than themselves.

- The benefits are undeniable:

  - **Unwavering support, no matter what.** You'll have people in your corner who will always have your back, even when you screw up.

  - **Opportunities and connections you wouldn't have otherwise.** You'll have access to a network of people who can help you achieve your goals and open doors you didn't even know existed.

  - **Accountability and motivation like you've never experienced.** You'll be surrounded by people pushing you to be your best and won't let you settle for mediocrity.

4. RECREATE

- This is where the real magic happens. A warrior constantly evolves, upgrading their armor and weapons, discarding the old, and embracing the new to become more effective in battle. That's what **Recreate** is all about. It's about killing the old you and unleashing the **WARRIOR** within.

- My journey is proof. I didn't just change my habits; I changed my identity. I killed the old Andy, who settled for less and unleashed the **WARRIOR** within. I embraced discomfort, pushed my limits, and never stopped learning.

- Here's how to recreate yourself:

  - **Identify and eliminate the bullshit.** What habits, beliefs, and behaviors are holding you back? Get rid of them. Don't be afraid to let go of the past.

  - **Embrace discomfort.** Step outside your comfort zone and challenge yourself to grow. The more uncomfortable you get, the stronger you become.

  - **Never stop learning.** Read books, listen to podcasts, attend seminars, and never stop seeking knowledge. The more you know, the more powerful you become.

- The rewards are worth the effort:

  - **Confidence that can't be shaken.** You'll feel more powerful and capable than ever before.

  - **Resilience that will blow your mind.** You'll be able to handle change and overcome challenges like a champ.

  - **A life that's aligned with your true purpose.** You'll live an authentic, fulfilling life that makes you want to jump out of bed every morning.

5. INTEGRATION

- This is about building a life, not just a business. A warrior understands that success isn't just about crushing it at work; it's about having a fulfilling and meaningful life in every area. That's what **Integration** is all about. It's about bringing your work and personal life together in a way that supports both.

- Jacqueline and I learned this the hard way. We brought our kids along on the journey. We built a business that aligned with our family values and found a way to integrate our work and life without sacrificing either. That's the **WARRIOR** way.

- Here's how to master work-life Integration:
  - **Don't try to balance; integrate.** Bring your family with you on your journey. Involve them in your business, share your goals, and make them part of your team.
  - **Be present wherever you are.** When you're at home, be at home. When you're at work, be at work. Don't let distractions steal your focus.
  - **Align your business goals with your personal values.** Ensure that what you do in the world is consistent with who you are and what you believe in.
- The benefits are life-changing:
  - **Fulfillment and happiness that's off the charts.** You'll be living a life that's both successful and meaningful, a life that makes you proud.
  - **Say goodbye to stress and burnout.** You'll be able to handle the demands of your life without feeling overwhelmed.
  - **A life of purpose that makes a difference.** You'll make a difference in the world and leave a legacy that matters.

6. OWNERSHIP

- This is about taking control. A warrior takes command of the battlefield, making decisions and taking responsibility for the outcome. They don't blame others; they own their shit. That's what **Ownership** is all about. It's about stepping up and being accountable for your life.
- I've always believed in this. From sleeping on mattresses to selling 70 cars monthly, I took 100% responsibility for my life. I didn't make excuses; I owned my choices and their consequences. That's the **WARRIOR'S** path to power.
- Here's how to take Ownership of your life:
  - **No more excuses.** Take 100% responsibility for your life, choices, and results. You are in control of your destiny.
  - **Focus on solutions, not problems.** Don't dwell on what's wrong; focus on what you can do to make it right.
  - **Embrace the power of your decisions.** Every choice has consequences, so make sure you're making choices that will lead you to the life you want.
- The payoff is massive:
  - **Confidence that can move mountains.** You'll feel more in control of your life and your destiny.

- **You'll become the architect of your own life.** You'll be able to create the life you want instead of letting life happen to you.

- **A sense of purpose that drives you forward.** You'll be living a life driven by your values and goals, a life that makes you want to get out of bed every morning.

7. REACH

- This is about leaving a legacy, brother. A warrior fights for a cause greater than themselves, leaving a legacy that inspires others. They're not just building a business; they're changing the world. That's what **Reach** is all about. It's about making an impact that extends beyond your own life.

- This is what drives me. I'm not just building a company; I'm building a movement. I inspire others to break free from their limitations and live their richest lives. That's the **WARRIOR'S** impact.

- Here's how to maximize your reach:

  - **Make an impact, influence others, and leave a legacy.** Find a way to give back to your community or the world. Mentor others, share your knowledge, and make a difference.

  - **Become a moral authority.** Live a life that inspires others to follow your example.

  - **Build an army of WARRIORS.** Train your team to be leaders, empower them to make a difference, and create a movement that will change the world.

- The rewards are immeasurable:

  - **Fulfillment and purpose that transcends your own life.** You'll be living a life that's both successful and meaningful, a life that makes a difference in the world.

  - **You'll feel connected and belong to something bigger than yourself.** You'll be part of something, changing the world and making a real difference.

  - **A legacy that outlives you.** You'll be leaving the world a better place than you found it. Your impact will continue to ripple outwards long after you're gone.

THE WARRIOR FRAMEWORK IN ACTION

This framework is a roadmap for Total Recreation, a guide to building a life of strength, purpose, and impact, just like The Elliott Group. By consistently applying the principles and actionable steps within each pillar, you can:

TRANSFORM YOUR BODY

Achieve peak physical fitness and unlock the mental and emotional benefits of a strong, healthy body. Become a walking billboard of human excellence.

MASTER YOUR MIND

Develop an unstoppable mindset, overcome limiting beliefs, and harness the power of your thoughts and actions. Become a master communicator and influencer.

BUILD UNBREAKABLE BONDS

Create an unrecruitable tribe of support, surround yourself with greatness, and experience the power of true brotherhood.

BECOME THE BEST VERSION OF YOURSELF

Shed the old you, unleash the **WARRIOR** within, and live a life aligned with your values and purpose.

ACHIEVE HOLISTIC SUCCESS

Integrate your work and life, create a fulfilling career, and build a legacy that matters.

Remember, the **WARRIOR Framework** is not a one-time fix but a lifelong journey of growth, transformation, and service. Embrace the challenge, trust the process, and never stop fighting for the life you deserve. Become the **WARRIOR** you were born to be.

This book is your call to arms, your invitation to a Total Recreation. It's the beginning of a journey to conquer mediocrity, shatter limitations, and unleash the WARRIOR within. But the journey doesn't end here. Scan the QR code below to download the Elliott Training Academy (ETA) app and access exclusive content, deeper dives into the WARRIOR Framework, and ongoing support from Andy and the Elliott Group team. Continue your transformation, connect with a community of like-minded warriors, and take your journey to the next level with ETA.

CHAPTER 1

THE DECISION TO CHANGE

There comes a defining moment in every person's life - a crossroads where you must choose between settling for mediocrity or rising to claim the extraordinary life you were meant to live. It's not always a dramatic, earth-shattering event. Sometimes, it's a quiet whisper in the dead of night, a nagging feeling that you're capable of more, a longing for something bigger than yourself. For me, that moment came in stages, a series of wake-up calls that shook me to my core and forced me to confront the man I had become.

The first tremor came from the woman who knows me best, my wife, Jacqueline. "Andy," she said, her voice laced with concern, "you're not living up to your potential." It was a warning, a shot across the bow, delivered with love but with a firmness that demanded my attention. Her words hit me like a gut punch. On the surface, life was good. I had a nice house, fancy cars, and a successful career in sales. But deep down, I knew something was off. I was chasing numbers, not dreams. I had become a prisoner of my success, trapped in a gilded cage of my own making.

Jacqueline has always been my biggest supporter, but she's also the first to call me out when I'm full of it. "You have a choice," she continued, her gaze unwavering. "You can either let your ego drive you down the wrong path, or you can take an honest look in the mirror and decide to become the winner you were born to be." She knew I had it in me, but I was standing at a fork in the road, and the wrong path was paved with ego and resistance. She allowed me to choose the growth path and become my best version.

That night, I stared at my reflection in the mirror, and for the first time, I didn't recognize the man staring back. Where was the driven, ambitious kid who used to hustle for every dollar? The one who dared to dream big and chase those dreams with reckless abandon? Somewhere along the way, comfort had crept in, slowly eroding my ambition and replacing it with complacency.

I had fallen victim to the "golden handcuff syndrome." I was making more money than I ever thought possible, but I hated my job. I felt like a cog in a machine, my soul slowly dying a little more each day. The things that used to motivate me—the thrill of the close and the satisfaction of crushing goals—had lost their luster. I was living a lie, a charade of success slowly eating away at me from the inside out.

Jacqueline could see it, too. She saw the frustration, the lack of fulfill- ment, the growing disconnect between who I was and who I wanted to be. She didn't sugarcoat it. "Don't get historical," she'd say, refusing to let me wallow in past mistakes or use them as an excuse for my current state. "From today forward, we're moving forward. The past is the past for a reason. The future is amazing. The past is… well, it's the past. Become your future self now."

Her words were a lifeline, pulling me out of the quicksand of my self- pity and pointing me toward a brighter horizon. She knew that change was possible, that I could break free from the chains of my past and become the man I was destined to be. And the most powerful thing? She believed in me, even when I struggled to believe in myself.

Deciding to change was challenging. It required swallowing my pride and admitting that I had made mistakes and strayed from the path I was meant to be on. It meant killing my ego, and opening myself up to the pos- sibility of becoming something more. But as Jacqueline reminded me, dwell- ing on the past would only keep me stuck. "The past is the past for a reason," she said. "From today forward, we're going to move forward. That's why most people never grow—they live in the past. But who you are now is not who you have to be. Become your future self now."

Her unwavering belief in me, even when I doubted myself, was the spark that ignited the fire within. Her love and support gave me the courage to bet on myself again, to dust off my dreams and chase them with everything I had. Together, we made a pact to face challenges head-on, knowing that each obstacle we overcame would only strengthen our bond and deepen our trust. We were in this together, a team, a force to be reckoned with.

We decided to embark on a journey of Total Recreation, a complete overhaul of our lives. We sold our house, downsized our possessions, and simplified our lives. We wanted to build something meaningful, to change our lives, and positively impact the world. We were breaking the mold, defying expectations, and creating a new path for ourselves and our families.

This journey wasn't just about us but about breaking free from the generational curses that had plagued our families for generations. We wanted to create a legacy of strength, resilience, and unwavering faith for our children, a legacy that would empower them to create their own extraordinary lives. We were bloodline breakers, pioneers forging a new path for future generations.

As we dove headfirst into this new chapter, I realized that lasting change requires more than willpower and good intentions. It demands a fundamental shift in identity. You must become comfortable with being uncomfortable and embrace the struggle as a necessary part of growth. You have to be willing to tear down the old to make way for the new, shed the skin of your former self, and emerge more robust, resilient, and aligned with your true purpose.

This transformation started with my mindset. I had to shift from being motivated to being driven. Motivated people, I realized, are easily derailed by obstacles. Driven people, on the other hand, are unstoppable forces of nature. They bulldoze through challenges fueled by an inner fire that can't be extinguished. They don't just want to succeed; they need to succeed. They are the ones who break records, shatter limitations, and redefine what's possible.

I had always been competitive, but now, my competition wasn't my colleagues or my rivals; it was the old me, the complacent me, the one who had settled for less than he could. I wanted to be so far ahead of my former self that I was in a league of my own. I envisioned a sales board with my name at the top, in a category all by itself, a testament to the power of transformation and relentless pursuit of excellence.

This drive wasn't about ego or arrogance; it was about proving to myself that I could achieve anything I set my mind to and break free from the limitations I had placed upon myself. It was about becoming the best version of myself, not for the accolades or the recognition, but for the satisfaction of knowing that I had pushed myself beyond what I thought was possible.

This new mindset permeated every aspect of my life. I set non-negotiables for myself, daily rituals that would push me beyond my comfort zone and build the discipline I needed to succeed. I committed to selling three cars daily or making 200 calls, no matter how long it took. And if I fell short of my sales goal, I punished myself with a three-mile run, a reminder that there were no excuses for mediocrity.

These daily rituals weren't about punishment; they were about accountability. They were about building the mental toughness and unwavering commitment I needed to achieve my goals. They were about proving to me that I was capable of more than I thought, could overcome any obstacle, and could accomplish any dream as long as I was willing to do the work.

This journey of Total Recreation wasn't just about external success but internal transformation. It was about developing a deep sense of self-worth, loving and accepting myself, flaws and all. It was about becoming the kind of man who could look in the mirror and be proud of the person staring back.

I realized that true confidence comes from keeping your promises to yourself, from doing what you say you're going to do, no matter what. It's about building a reputation with yourself, a track record of integrity, and an unwavering commitment to growth.

This commitment extended to my relationships as well. Jacqueline and I became an actual power couple, supporting each other's dreams, holding each other accountable, and celebrating each other's victories. We learned to communicate openly and honestly, to be vulnerable with each other, and to trust each other implicitly. We were a team united in pursuing a richer, more fulfilling life, not just for ourselves but also for our children.

We taught our kids the same values of hard work, resilience, and unwavering faith. We wanted them to know that they could achieve anything they set their minds to and that they didn't have to be limited by their circumstances or past. We wanted them to be bloodline breakers, to create a new legacy of success and fulfillment for future generations.

THE RENEGADE PATH TO MORAL AUTHORITY

This decision to change and embark on this journey of Total Recreation was also about embracing the renegade within. It was about challenging societal norms and forging our path, even if it meant breaking the rules. We weren't going to let the expectations of others dictate our lives. We were going to define success on our own terms and build a life reflecting our values and vision.

One of our most radical decisions was incorporating fitness into our sales training. Everyone told us it wouldn't work, that corporate clients wouldn't do it. But we knew that physical and mental strength were inextricably linked. We believed that pushing our team members physically could help them unlock mental toughness and resilience that would translate into massive success in sales and life.

And you know what? We were right. Our unconventional approach attracted top talent and created a culture of discipline, accountability, and unwavering commitment within our team. We weren't just building salespeople; we were building leaders. We were creating a movement, a brotherhood of individuals committed to becoming the best versions of themselves in every area of their lives.

This renegade spirit, this willingness to challenge the status quo, was also about cultivating moral authority. It wasn't about preaching or forcing our beliefs on others. It was about living our values authentically and powerfully, and it inspired others to raise their standards. It was about becoming the example, the living embodiment of what's possible when you commit to Total Recreation.

People were drawn to our moral authority not because we were perfect or had all the answers but because we were real. We were transparent about our struggles, failures, and journey of transformation. And that authenticity and vulnerability created a level of trust and respect that no amount of marketing or hype could ever replicate.

THE POWER OF COMPRESSED TIMEFRAMES

This journey of Total Recreation wasn't about slow, incremental change. We were on a mission to achieve in months, which most people take years to accomplish. We embraced the power of compressed timeframes, setting audacious 90-day goals that forced us to push our limits and operate at a level of intensity we never thought possible.

We knew that if we wanted to break free from the patterns of our past and create a new legacy, we had to accelerate our growth. We couldn't afford to waste time on distractions or self-doubt. We had to compress our time-lines and make every single day count.

This approach wasn't for the faint of heart. It required discipline, focus, and a willingness to embrace discomfort. But the results were undeniable. In those 90-day sprints, we achieved what most people couldn't accomplish in years. We shattered limiting beliefs, broke through barriers, and created momentum that propelled us forward with unstoppable force.

This commitment to compressed timeframes was also about maximizing our impact on the world. We knew that the more quickly we could achieve our goals, the more people we could help, and the more lives we could transform. It was about creating a ripple effect of positive change extending far beyond our lives.

THE JOURNEY BEGINS WITH A DECISION AND A FRAMEWORK FOR ACTION

The decision to change is the most crucial step on this journey of Total Recreation. It's the spark that ignites the fire, the catalyst that propels you forward. It's about recognizing that you're worthy of an extraordinary life and committing to becoming the best, most powerful version of yourself.

But to navigate this journey successfully, you need more than just a decision; you need a framework for action. You need a battle plan. And that's where the **WARRIOR Framework** comes in.

The **WARRIOR Framework**, which we'll dive deep into throughout this book, is the blueprint for building an unstoppable mindset and achieving the life you were meant to live. It's about:

WORKOUT
Activating your body and mind for the challenges ahead.

AWARENESS
Knowing yourself—your strengths, weaknesses, and patterns—with brutal honesty.

RELATIONSHIPS
Building an unbreakable tribe of support, surrounding yourself with those who elevate and challenge you.

RECREATE
To unleash the **WARRIOR** within, shedding the old you, the limitations and beliefs that no longer serve you.

INTEGRATION
Living a life of seamless integration, where your work and personal life fuel each other, not compete.

OWNERSHIP
Taking 100% responsibility for your choices, actions, and outcomes. No excuses.

REACH
Living a life of impact, influence, and legacy, striving to make a difference in the world that extends beyond yourself.

This is the **WARRIOR'S** path. It's a journey of transformation, growth, and unwavering commitment. And it all starts with a single, powerful decision: the decision to change.

CHAPTER 1 TAKEAWAYS

- **The Decision to Change:** This is where it all begins. It's a commitment to yourself, a declaration that you're no longer willing to settle for mediocrity.

- **The WARRIOR Framework:** Your roadmap and battle plan for achieving Total Recreation. Embrace, embody, and use it to guide you on your journey.

You've decided to change and begun to understand the WARRIOR Framework. Now, take the next step in your journey toward Total Recreation. Deepen your understanding and implement these principles by watching our "Seeking Approval From Others" video at Elliott Training Academy (ETA). Scan the QR code to watch the video to continue your transformation.

CHAPTER 2

BREAKING THE BLOODLINE

Have you ever felt like no matter how hard you work, you can't seem to break free from the patterns and limitations that have defined your family for generations? Maybe your parents struggled financially and could never get ahead, no matter how many hours they put in. Or perhaps addiction, divorce, or negativity are common themes that have followed your relatives like a dark cloud.

I know exactly how that feels because I've been there. Growing up, failure felt like it was woven into my DNA. From a young age, I watched my family members repeat the same self-defeating cycles repeatedly, never quite able to break free and create something better.

Listen, let's talk about something real—your Bloodline. No, I'm not discussing some mystical family tree or ancient secrets. I'm talking about the invisible script you inherited. It's the beliefs and behaviors passed down through the generations. It's the DNA of your upbringing, shaping your thoughts, habits, and, ultimately, your life.

For some, it's a legacy of success, a foundation built on hard work and ambition. But for many, it's a chain holding them back, a cycle of negativity, poverty, or broken dreams. Maybe you grew up thinking small and were told you'd be lucky to get a decent job and keep your head down. Perhaps you saw your parents struggle, their dreams put off or shattered, and you accepted that as your fate. That's the Bloodline talking, whispering limiting beliefs in your ear. Children who grow up in poverty are more likely to experience poverty as adults. In the United States, about 40% of children who grow up in poverty will remain poor as adults. This is due to a lack of access to quality education, healthcare, and social capital, making it difficult to break the cycle.

But here's the thing - your past doesn't have to define your future. You can break the Bloodline and create a new legacy for yourself and your loved ones. It all starts with understanding the patterns that have held you back, facing your childhood demons, and deciding to forge a new path. This is where Total Recreation comes in.

TOTAL RECREATION:
REWRITING YOUR DNA

Total Recreation isn't just about achieving success; it's about becoming the architect of your own life. It's about taking ownership of your thoughts, beliefs, and actions and consciously creating a new reality that aligns with your deepest values and aspirations.

Think of it as rewriting your DNA, shedding the limitations of your past, and stepping into the fullness of your potential. It's a journey of self-discovery, transformation, and liberation, where you break free from the chains of your Bloodline and emerge as the hero of your own story. The Adverse Childhood Experiences (ACE) Study found that nearly two-thirds of adults reported experiencing at least one type of adverse childhood experience, and those with higher ACE scores were more likely to experience health problems, mental illness, and substance abuse. This is because childhood trauma can have a lasting impact on brain development, leading to difficulties with emotional regulation, impulse control, and forming healthy relationships. Even more concerning, research suggests that traumatic experiences can lead to epigenetic changes that are passed down to future generations, potentially increasing the risk of mental health problems and other health issues.

THE FOUR PILLARS OF TOTAL RECREATION

Total Recreation is built on four fundamental pillars that will guide you on your journey to breaking the Bloodline and creating a life of purpose, abundance, and fulfillment:

1. UNSCREW YOURSELF

This is about taking radical responsibility for your life. It's about recognizing that you are the author of your story, the creator of your reality. Stop blaming your past, circumstances, or others for your current situation. Own your choices, your mistakes, and your successes. When you unscrew yourself, you empower yourself to change anything.

2. RECREATE YOUR IDENTITY

Your identity is the story you tell yourself about yourself. It's shaped by your past experiences, beliefs, and self-perception. To break free from your Bloodline, you must consciously choose to recreate your identity. Identify the limiting beliefs that hold you back and replace them with empowering truths. Step into a new version of yourself that aligns with your vision for the future.

3. BECOME UNRECRUITABLE

This is about building a life so fulfilling and aligned with your purpose that no money or external validation could lure you away. It's about creating a business, a team, and a lifestyle that reflects your deepest values and passions. When you become unrecruitable, you achieve true freedom and independence.

4. LIVE A LIFE THAT COUNTS

This is about making a difference and leaving a legacy beyond your lifetime. It's about using your gifts, talents, and resources to serve others and positively impact your community and the world at large. When you live a life that counts, you experience fulfillment and satisfaction that money can't buy.

BLOODLINE BREAKERS:
OVERCOMING GENERATIONAL PATTERNS

One of the most powerful things you can do to transform your life is to become what I call a "bloodline breaker." This means looking hard at your family's beliefs, behaviors, and limitations and consciously choosing to do things differently.

Many people talk about DNA as if this permanent thing dictates who we are and what we're capable of. They use it as an excuse, saying things like "I can't start a business because no one in my family is an entrepreneur" or "I'll never have a good relationship because my parents got divorced."

But here's the truth - your DNA doesn't define your destiny. Sure, you might have inherited certain tendencies or challenges, but you also have the power to overcome them. You get to decide what kind of life you want to create, regardless of what your family history might suggest.

Look at my wife Jacqueline and I. We both had tough childhoods that could have easily set us up for a life of struggle and limitation. Jacqueline grew up in a rough part of town, surrounded by gang violence and dysfunction. Her parents were the first in their families to get divorced, and she always felt like everyone pitied her.

As for me, let me tell you about my Bloodline. My childhood wasn't glamorous. My mom struggled with alcoholism and left when I was just two. My dad, the hardest working man I knew, did his best to provide for me and my siblings, but supervision wasn't a priority. We had a broken family, zero money, and even less hope.

Growing up in that environment, I was programmed to think small. Get a job, stay out of jail—that was the mantra. I scraped by in school, barely graduating, a testament to everyone's low expectations. I had no grand vision for my life, no burning desire for anything more than just getting by. That was the legacy I inherited, the DNA of my upbringing.

But despite our difficult beginnings, Jacqueline and I refused to let our pasts define us. We decided to break free from the limiting beliefs and patterns that had held our families back for generations. We created a new legacy built on hard work, determination, and unwavering faith in ourselves and God.

And you know what? It was really challenging. Breaking free from your Bloodline takes guts. It means being willing to do things differently than everyone around you. It means facing your fears, doubts, and insecurities head-on. It means sacrificing comfort in the short term for the sake of your long-term vision.

But I can tell you from personal experience that it's so freaking worth it. Everything changes when you break free from your old patterns and start living on your own terms. You begin seeing obstacles as opportunities. You find the courage to take bold risks. You develop an unshakeable faith in your ability to create the life you want, no matter what anyone else says or thinks.

FACING YOUR CHILDHOOD DEMONS

Of course, breaking the Bloodline is easier said than done. One of the biggest challenges many face is overcoming the painful experiences and limiting beliefs we developed in childhood.

Maybe you grew up in poverty and internalized the idea that you'd never be successful. Perhaps you were bullied or rejected and started believing you weren't good enough. Or maybe you witnessed your parents' dysfunctional relationship and swore you'd never let yourself fall in love.

Whatever your specific story, those early experiences shape our beliefs and behaviors well into adulthood—usually without us even realizing it. We carry around unconscious scripts that tell us what we can and can't do and what we do and don't deserve.

Breaking free from your Bloodline means facing those demons head-on. It means revisiting your childhood wounds and allowing yourself to feel the pain, anger, and sadness you might have buried long ago. It means challenging the beliefs you developed way back when and deciding which ones serve you and which ones need to go.

This isn't always a comfortable process. In fact, it can be downright terrifying at times. But in my experience, facing your demons is one of the most liberating things you can do. When you shine a light on your shadows and confront them directly, they lose their power over you. You begin to see that you are much stronger and more resilient than you ever realized.

Jacqueline is a perfect example of this. For years, she struggled with feelings of inadequacy that stemmed from her difficult childhood. She believed she would never have the close-knit family she longed for because dysfunction was all she knew. She was cold and closed-off, always trying to protect herself from getting hurt again.

But something shifted as she examined those old wounds and questioned her childhood beliefs. She realized that her past didn't have to dictate her future. She could break the cycle and create something new—a loving, supportive family.

It wasn't an overnight transformation by any means. Jacqueline had to put in the hard work of healing her trauma, learning to open her heart, and building Trust where there had only been pain before. But little by little, she recreated her DNA and rewrote her story. Today, she is an incredible mother, wife, and leader who inspires others to break free from their own limiting patterns.

Your journey will look different than Jacqueline's or mine. But no matter what challenges you might carry from your childhood, know you have the strength to overcome them. With God by your side and a commitment to doing the inner work, you can emerge from your pain as the hero of your story.

BREAKING THE BLOODLINE IN ACTION

At 18, a friend's brother offered me a chance to sell cars. I was a terrible speaker, stuttered, and had zero experience. But that $5,000 a month he promised? That sounded like a fortune to a kid who'd never held more than five bucks in his hand.

That was the day my life changed forever. It wasn't easy. I had to fight tooth and nail for every sale, overcome my fear of rejection, and learn how to connect with people. But I was hungry, driven by a force I didn't fully understand then. It was the fire of breaking the Bloodline, the desire to create something different, something better than what I was handed.

Within a year, I had a new house, a Corvette, and more money than I ever thought possible. Sales became my escape, my ticket to a different life. But it was more than just closing deals; it was about mastering my mind, conquering my limiting beliefs, and proving to myself that I was capable of more than anyone, even myself, believed.

Breaking the Bloodline is about confronting those ingrained patterns, those voices whispering, "You're not good enough," or "You'll never amount to anything." It's about recognizing that your past doesn't define your future and that you can choose a different path.

Here's the deal: breaking free from those invisible chains requires conscious effort. It's about rewiring your mind and replacing those limiting beliefs with empowering truths. It's about taking ownership of your life and making choices that align with the legacy you want to create.

CHAPTER 2 TAKEAWAYS

- **Your Bloodline Isn't Your Destiny:** You can choose a different path, regardless of your family history.

- **Unscrew Yourself:** Take radical responsibility for your life and stop blaming your past.

- **Recreate Your Identity:** Challenge limiting beliefs and step into a new, empowered version of yourself.

- **Face Your Demons:** Confront your childhood wounds and heal from past traumas.

- **Embrace the Power of Total Recreation:** Commit to rewriting your DNA and creating a life of purpose, abundance, and fulfillment.

You've learned that your bloodline isn't your destiny and that you have the power to unscrew yourself from the past. Now, it's time to take concrete steps towards recreating your identity and facing your demons. Watch our "Breaking Curses" video at Elliott Training Academy (ETA). Scan the QR code to watch the video to deepen your understanding of breaking free from limiting beliefs and past traumas and continue your journey toward Total Recreation.

-----------------------ᗺᗯᗺ-

THE SACRIFICE FOR SUCCESS

Success doesn't come easy. It's not handed to you on a silver platter. No, if you want to achieve greatness or build an extraordinary life, you have to be willing to make sacrifices. You have to be ready to give up comfort, convenience, and the path of least resistance. Because here's the truth - there's no growth in the comfort zone. There's no transformation without pain. If you want to become the person you were born to be, the person God designed you to be, buckle up. It's going to be one hell of a ride.

Let's talk about sacrifice. It's not the kind of throwing a goat on an altar—although sometimes, building a business can feel that intense. I'm talking about the conscious, occasionally tricky choices we make to achieve something bigger than ourselves. This is where the **WARRIOR** within you starts to emerge. Remember, a true **WARRIOR** understands that Ownership means taking control of their destiny; sometimes, that means making tough choices.

Most folks think sacrifice is about giving something up—it's a loss. But that's a scared mindset. Total Recreation flips that script. Sacrifice isn't about loss. It's about investment. It's about planting seeds for a future harvest that'll blow your mind. It's about embracing the **WARRIOR** principle of Reach, understanding that your sacrifices today are building towards a legacy that matters. This concept is backed by research on delayed gratification, exemplified in the Stanford Marshmallow Experiment (Mischel, 1972). Children who could delay gratification and resist immediate rewards for a larger reward later exhibited greater success in various aspects of their lives. They understood that sometimes, you must sacrifice now to reap greater benefits later.

Now, this ain't some prosperity gospel BS. This is about looking opportunity dead in the eye and having the guts to say, "You know what? I'm willing to put in the work, even if it means getting uncomfortable and making tough calls." This is about tapping into the **WARRIOR'S** spirit of working, pushing past your limits, and building the mental and physical resilience to conquer any challenge. In her research on grit, Angela Duckworth emphasizes the importance of passion and perseverance in achieving long-term goals (Duckworth, 2016). This grit often requires making sacrifices and pushing through challenges to reach the desired outcome.

I know this firsthand. I've lived it. When Jacqueline and I started building our company, we had to make serious sacrifices. We were all in. Remember that "million-dollar house" Jacqueline mentioned? The one with the fancy plans and the big dreams attached? Yeah, we were that close to breaking ground. Imagine sprawling rooms, a view for days, and maybe one of those fancy espresso machines. We could practically taste it.

But then something shifted. We asked ourselves, "What's the cost of this dream?" not just the financial cost, although that was a big one, but the cost of our time, energy, and focus. We were pouring everything into building this business, this movement, and something had to give. This was a moment of profound Awareness, a realization that our Relationships and shared vision were more important than any material possession. Every choice comes with an opportunity cost—the value of the next best alternative we forgo. By choosing to invest in our business, we were consciously sacrificing the comfort and security of that dream house for the potential of building something extraordinary.

So, we made a decision. We chose to sell that dream house, that symbol of comfort and security, and poured every dime, every ounce of energy, into our vision. We downsized to a small rental and created what I like to call our "war room."

There was no fancy furniture, no distractions—just plastic tables, computers humming, and mattresses on the floor. It was raw and gritty, but it was laser-focused. We were all in, betting on ourselves and our dreams. This was our Workout, our training ground for greatness. We were stripping away the excess, honing our focus, and building the mental toughness required to win.

You might be thinking, "Andy, that's insane. Why would you put your family through that?" But see, that's the thing. We didn't see it as a hardship. We saw it as an opportunity to grow closer as a family, teach our kids the value of hard work and resilience, strip away all the excess, and focus on what mattered—each other and our dreams. This was Integration in action, aligning our family life with our mission and building a legacy together.

Now, some folks, even family, might have called us crazy. But we had a "no complaining" rule. We knew the power of protecting our vision, of not letting doubt creep in. This was our journey, our sacrifice, and we owned every minute of it. This unwavering belief, this refusal to be deterred, is the hallmark of a true **WARRIOR**.

And let me tell you, those weren't easy days. We were working like animals, hustling, grinding, pushing ourselves to the limit. Jacqueline was a force of nature, cooking up beans and rice twenty different ways, making sure we were fueled and focused.

I'll be honest: There were times when we looked at each other, exhausted, and wondered, "What the hell are we doing?" But then we'd remind ourselves why we started this whole thing. It wasn't about the money, not really. It was about building something bigger than ourselves, about leaving a legacy. This is the essence of Reach: understanding that our sacrifices were not just for us but for something much greater.

It was about proving to ourselves and everyone who doubted us that we could achieve anything we set our minds to. And let me tell you, there's a power in that kind of conviction that'll move mountains.

Now, I'm not saying you have to sell all your worldly possessions and sleep on the floor to be successful. But you must be willing to let go of anything holding you back. Anything that's not serving your highest purpose. That might mean saying no to nights out with the boys so you can put in extra hours on your business. It might mean skipping that fancy vacation so you can invest in a course to learn a new skill. It might mean dropping toxic friends who don't support your vision. Building a powerful **WARRIOR** network means surrounding yourself with people who uplift and inspire you, not drag you down.

The point is that sacrifice is necessary for growth. You can't level up without giving something up. But here's the key - you have to make strategic sacrifices. You can't just throw away everything that matters to you in the name of success. You have to be intentional. You have to weigh the costs and the benefits. You must ask yourself, "Is this sacrifice getting me closer to my goal? Is it aligned with my values? Is it worth the price I'm paying?" The Pareto Principle, also known as the 80/20 rule, can be valuable for making these strategic sacrifices. This principle suggests that 80% of your results come from 20% of your efforts. By identifying and focusing on the 20% of activities that yield the most significant results, you can make strategic sacrifices, eliminate time-wasting tasks, and achieve greater efficiency and success.

When Jacqueline and I decided to sell our house and move into that tiny 1-bedroom house, we didn't do it on a whim. We had a plan. We knew that by cutting our living expenses, we could pour more money into our business. We knew that by simplifying our lives, we could focus more on what mattered. And we knew that by involving our kids in the journey, we could teach them priceless lessons about chasing your dreams.

But we also set boundaries. We didn't work 24/7. We made sure to carve out quality time with each other and our kids daily. We didn't neglect our health or let our marriage suffer. Because at the end of the day, no amount of success is worth losing the people you love. No achievement can fill the void of a broken relationship or a neglected soul.

You might think, "Andy, I get it; sacrifice is important, but how do I know what to sacrifice? How do I find that balance without losing everything?" This is where the **WARRIOR'S** Awareness comes into play. You need to know yourself, your values, and your non-negotiables.

Here's the deal: there's no one-size-fits-all answer. But I can tell you this: it starts with clarifying what truly matters to you. What are your non-negotiables? What are you willing to fight for, to go to war for? For me, it's my faith, my family, and my health. Those are the foundations of my life, and I won't compromise them for anything. Think about what matters most to you and write it down. Let that be your guiding light.

Once you know your "why," the sacrifices become clearer. They're not losses anymore; they're strategic investments in your future. And trust me, the more strategic you are with your sacrifices, the less you'll feel like you're giving anything up.

Maybe it means saying "no" to distractions, to those shiny objects that suck your time and energy. Perhaps it means having uncomfortable conversations, setting boundaries, and prioritizing your vision.

Or it could mean selling that dream house and sleeping on mattresses for a while. Because when you're hungry and have something to prove, you tap into a level of drive and determination that most folks will never know.

And that, my friends, is where the magic happens. That's when you become the person you were always meant to be, who can achieve anything you set your mind to.

Now, I want to be clear - sacrifice doesn't mean suffering. In fact, true success should feel good. It should light you up from the inside out. But the reality is, to get to that place of joy and fulfillment, you will have to stretch yourself. You're going to have to do things that scare you. You're going to have to trade short-term pleasure for long-term gain.

And that's not always easy. I often wished to kick back and chill in my fancy house with my fancy cars. Times when I wanted to take the easy road, the known path. But deep down, I knew that wasn't what I was made for. I knew I was called to something greater. And I was willing to pay the price to get there.

So let me ask you: What are you willing to sacrifice for your dreams? What are you ready to let go of to become the person you know you can be? What short-term discomforts are you willing to endure for long-term joy and impact?

For you, waking up an hour earlier every day to study before your day job. It could be volunteering your time and talents to a cause you believe in, even when you're tired and busy.

Whatever it is, know that every sacrifice you make is planting a seed. A seed of discipline, of focus, of resilience. A seed that will one day bloom into a life beyond your wildest dreams. A life of passion, purpose, and unwavering faith.

But you must be willing to plant those seeds, even when you can't yet see the harvest. You have to trust the process, even when it's painful. You must keep showing up, even when you feel like giving up.

Most of all, you must surround yourself with people who cheer you on, challenge you to grow, and pick you up when you fall. People who understand the price of greatness and are willing to pay it alongside you. People who share your values, vision, and relentless drive. This is the power of the **WARRIOR'S** Relationships, the unbreakable bonds that fuel your journey.

That's what Jacqueline and I did. We became an unshakable team, a united front. We pushed, believed in each other, and held each other accountable. And when things got tough, we locked arms and weathered the storm together.

That's the power of a true bloodline breaker—someone who looks at a challenge and says, "Bring it on." Someone hungry for growth, impact, and a life that leaves a legacy. Someone who understands that sacrifice is the price of admission to the life they were born to live.

Remember, this journey is about more than just success; it's about transformation. It's about killing off the old you who's afraid to sacrifice, dream big, and step into a truly extraordinary life. This is the essence of Recreate, shedding the skin of your past and forging a new, more powerful identity.

So, ask yourself: What will you sacrifice to create the life you've always wanted? The truth is, the only thing standing between you and your dreams is your willingness to pay the price. And trust me, the reward is worth every damn penny.

As we wrap up this chapter, I want to leave you with a challenge. I want you to look hard at your life and ask yourself, "What's one thing you can sacrifice this week to get closer to your dreams?" It doesn't have to be huge. It could be as simple as skipping your favorite TV show to read a book instead or saying no to a night out so you can work on your business plan.

But I want you to make that sacrifice with intention. I want you to offer it up as an act of faith, an investment in your future. And then I want you to keep going. Day by day, week by week, keep making those strategic sacrifices. Keep pushing yourself out of your comfort zone. Keep betting on your God-given potential.

Because on the other hand, sacrifice is a life beyond your wildest imagination. A life of true success, true joy, true impact. A life where you wake up every day excited to serve, give, and grow. A life where you look back on all those sacrifices and say, "damn, it was so worth it."

That's the life Jacqueline and I are living now—the life we bled, fought, and believed in, the life we were willing to sleep on mattresses for.

And if a couple of broke kids that came out of Oklahoma can do it, so can you. You've got what it takes. You've got the hunger, the drive, the untapped potential. All you need is the courage to let go of the old you and embrace the new.

So let this chapter be your wake-up call, your invitation to a life unleashed, and your permission slip to make the sacrifices your soul is longing to make.

And know that every step of the way, you've got a God who loves you, a community who believes in you, and a power inside you that can't be stopped.

So what do you say? Are you ready to sacrifice for success? Are you ready to join the army of bloodline breakers?

If so, then let's get to work. There are mattresses to sleep on, dreams to chase, and a world to change.

And we're just getting started.

CHAPTER 3 TAKEAWAYS

- **Reframe Sacrifice Through Ownership and Reach:** Sacrifice isn't about loss but strategic investment, driven by your Ownership of your choices and your desire for Reach, a legacy that matters. It's about letting go of the good to make room for the great. Shift your mindset from scarcity to abundance, knowing that every sacrifice is planting a seed for future success.

- **Clarity of Priorities Through Awareness:** Successful sacrifice starts with crystal clarity on your non-negotiables, fueled by deep Awareness of your values. What are your core values and unshakable priorities? Let these be your guiding light and decision-making filter. Sacrifice what matters least for what matters most.

- **Communicate and Collaborate Through Relationships:** Sacrifice is rarely a solo journey. Bring your loved ones along for the ride, building the Relationships that will sustain you. Communicate your vision, listen to their concerns, and make them feel included. When sacrifice becomes a team effort, a shared mission, it's no longer a burden—it's a bonding experience.

- **Embrace the Stretch as Your Workout:** Sacrifice will stretch you. It will push you out of your comfort zone and challenge your limits. Embrace this discomfort as your Workout, knowing that this is where growth happens. On the other side of every stretch is a stronger, wiser, more capable you.

- Eyes on the Prize, Fueled by Reach: When the sacrifices feel heavy, keep your eyes on the dream that drives you. Let your vision be your motivation, your north star, fueled by your desire for Reach. Remind yourself daily why you started and what you're fighting for. Let that fire fuel you through the tough times.

- **Trust the Process, Unleash Your WARRIOR:** Sacrifice is an act of faith—faith in yourself, your resilience, and a higher purpose. Trust that every sacrifice, every seed planted, is part of a larger plan. Surrender your doubts and lean into the journey, unleashing the warrior within, knowing that growth is never a straight line but always leads to greatness.

- **Find Your Tribe, Build Your Relationships:** Surround yourself with people who understand the price of greatness and are willing to pay it alongside you. Find mentors, partners, and a community of like-minded dreamers and doers. Let their support uplift you, their belief embolden you, and their love sustains you. This is the power of Relationships, the foundation of your **WARRIOR** tribe.

These sacrificial principles have guided my journey, from sleeping on mattresses to living my God-sized dreams. But they're not just my principles—they're a blueprint for anyone ready to let go of mediocrity and step into a life of meaning.

So take these lessons, these hard-won truths, and make them your own. Start small, but start now. Choose one thing to sacrifice this week, then another, then another. Let each sacrifice strengthen your resolve, deepen your faith, and propel you closer to the life you were born to live.

Remember, on the other side of sacrifice is a life beyond your wildest dreams—a life of passion, purpose, and unwavering faith—a life where every sacrifice becomes a badge of honor, a testament to your unbreakable spirit.

That life is waiting for you. All you have to do is let go of the old and embrace the new. All you have to do is decide that you are worth the sacrifice.

So, what will you sacrifice for success? What will be the first step on your own journey of Total Recreation? The choice is yours, but know this: every great story, every legacy that lasts, starts with a single sacrifice. Make yours today, and watch your life transform in ways you never thought possible.

You've explored the power of strategic sacrifice, understanding how Ownership, Reach, Awareness, and Relationships play crucial roles. Now, delve deeper into the practical application of these principles. Watch our "Heaviest Burden" video at Elliott Training Academy (ETA). Scan the QR code to watch the video and discover how to make sacrifices that empower your journey.

CHAPTER 4

WORK-LIFE INTEGRATION

BUILDING YOUR EMPIRE BRICK BY BRICK, TOGETHER

Listen up because this chapter is crucial. We're talking about building an empire, not just a business. And let me tell you something: You can't build anything worthwhile without a solid foundation. In the game of life, that foundation is your family, your relationships, and the people you love and who love you back. This is the essence of the Integration pillar in the **WARRIOR Framework** - creating a life where your work fuels your personal life and vice versa.

I used to think success was all about crushing it at work, making the bank, and being a boss. And don't get me wrong—those things are important. But they mean nothing if you're coming home to an empty shell, a family that barely knows you, and a relationship running on fumes.

That was me. I was so focused on building my business that I forgot to nurture the most important one: my relationship with my wife, Jacqueline. I was all about that Ownership in my business, but I wasn't owning my responsibility to my family.

Now, Jacqueline, she's a force of nature. Strong, driven, a total badass in her own right. And she believed in me, even when I doubted myself. But I wasn't giving her what she deserved: my presence, energy, and love. After a long day of conquering the business world, I gave her the leftovers, the scraps of my attention.

I remember there was a time when my wife walked into a sales meeting that I was having with my team back when I was in the automotive industry. And I was giving them the sales meeting of a lifetime. Motivating the hell out of them. And my wife goes, "Man, I wish I could get some of that. Man, if the kids and I could get some of that, Andy, damn. I can only imagine how they feel right now."

I sat there. And I was like... The question I asked myself was, who am I trying to please? So why don't you ask that question? Who are you trying to please? You won't break your bloodline if you're trying to please the wrong people. You're not. No. Right now, you need to decide who you want to take care of in your life. And I want you to be good to everybody. But you need to put these people that you want to take care of into a category and make sure these people get special energy and they get taken care of. Okay.

That night, Jacqueline sat me down and said, "Andy, me and the kids have learned to live without you."

Man, those words hit me like a ton of bricks. It was a wake-up call, a slap in the face from the universe, a sign from God that I was heading down the wrong path. I was neglecting the Relationships that mattered most. That's when I realized that true success isn't about compartmentalizing your life, keeping work and family separate. It's about integrating those two worlds and building your empire brick by brick. It's about understanding that the energy you bring to your Workout should fuel your entire life, not just your business.

Research backs this up. Studies show that employees who feel their employers care about their well-being are more engaged and productive (Gallup, 2023). Companies with high employee engagement experience increased profitability, productivity, customer loyalty, and lower turnover rates. Additionally, employees with access to flexible work arrangements and work-life balance initiatives report higher levels of job satisfaction, commitment to their employers, and overall well-being (Society for Human Resource Management, 2020).

Jacqueline and I are a team. We always have been, even when we were butting heads, fighting for control, and trying to figure out this crazy dance of marriage and entrepreneurship. We learned that power couples aren't about one person outshining the other. It's about alignment, having shared goals, pushing each other to improve, and becoming a united front against the world.

This is super important. For many of you, there are many things you don't know about us, and I want to share them all with you. My wife and I like to be vulnerable with people because we're all human beings. Jacqueline and I, we're just normal, just like you. But what we did was make a decision to change. And there were a lot of things that we needed to change that. Unfortunately, my dumb ass waited too long to do it.

So, how did we go from a relationship on the brink to a power couple building a legacy? It wasn't easy, but here's the blueprint, built on the foundation of the **WARRIOR Framework**:

HONESTY HOUR

We got real with each other. There was no more sugarcoating or sweeping things under the rug. We had some tough conversations, aired our grievances, and, most importantly, listened to each other's needs.

Jacqueline's perspective is crucial here. She shared, "So I'm going to go over some of the things because a lot of people ask me questions and are like, 'Hey, you know how did Andy get his energy?' or 'How can I keep, you know, this drive?' or 'How can I maintain this and kind of just keep scaling in my business or with my family or continue to be a better person and not go back?' This call is so special and important to so many people because I just want to tell you that we went through so much. I identified myself in such a different way in the past, and I'm going to go over some of the things that I've done in the past; I had to break my bloodline, break my DNA, and break all these generational curses to be with a man like Andy, and also Andy had to break so many to be who he is."

SHARED VISION

We defined what we wanted our life to look like personally and professionally. We wrote down our goals, discussed our dreams, and ensured we were on the same page. This wasn't just about building a business; it was about creating a legacy, a key element of the Reach pillar.

I love that my wife was standing next to me. You know what she told me? I remember this one event in 2019 when I got into self-development. I quit my job. 2020, I'm sitting here starting a new journey. I go to this event. And I said, I want to be the number one sales trainer in the world. As a matter of fact, I take that back. I said I wanted to be the world's number-one automotive sales trainer. And my wife is sitting next to me. Now, this is where it's important. You need to look to your wife. When a husband and wife accomplish a goal together, they become unstoppable and dangerous. That's why there's power in a relationship.

But I want to tell you something. I looked over. My wife interrupted me while the speaker was talking. And she said, "No, not automotive." She said, "In the world. We want to build the world's number one sales training program." And he said, "Whoa." He said, "That's crazy."

UNIFIED FRONT

We decided to attack life as a team. It was no longer "me versus you." It was "us against the world." We had each other's backs, supported each other's ambitions, and celebrated each other's wins. We were building our Relationships into an unrecruitable tribe.

I'm talking about us building it together because I learned how to make money very young, and so did Jacqueline. Still, until we got together and joined forces, we knew that we needed to go along the same journey we were able to build something sustainable. So, for those of you that I see as couples doing it together, you are on the right path because, at first, Jacqueline and I, since we're both alphas, were fighting against each other. And if you're a man or a woman, and you're very high-driven and do very well at your job, you're like most people out there. You're going to get a job, and you're going to get married, and you're going to have your family fight you along the way unless you're on the same page.

FAMILY FIRST

We consciously decided to put our family at the center of everything we do. We involve our kids in our work, teach them about business, and show them that success is more than just money; it's about building something meaningful together. This is the heart of Integration - making family a part of your journey, not separate from it.

If you don't take care of your wife, someone else will. If you don't take care of your kids, someone else will. My immediate family drives me... my blood family moving forward with me, my wife, and my children; that's my new bloodline, guys. I'm recreating my DNA. You say, "Andy, what does that mean?" That means I don't give a crap about chromosomes. I don't care about DNA. I don't care about any of that. I'm building a new DNA. What is my

DNA? Whatever the hell is in my head, I'm creating that in my bloodline now, and that is our legacy - that's what our family lives by. Not any crap that's happened in the past.

My wife. I will be present. All the time. When I'm with my wife. I will show her. Not tell her how much I love her. I will show her. I will be with her. I'll be present. I will show my family massive amounts of love. No matter what. My children. No one's going to be my kid's hero. But me. Period. End of story. Every freaking day. I have built a life where my children are with me everywhere.

That meant making some tough choices. We sold our million-dollar house, downsized to a smaller place, and, for a while, lived a much simpler life. But you know what? We didn't complain, not once. We knew it was a temporary sacrifice for the greater good. We were building something extraordinary and doing it together as a family.

And let me tell you, the rewards have been immeasurable. Our relationship is stronger than ever, our kids are thriving, and our business is exploding because we're not just building a company; we're building a legacy.

One story that really illustrates the power of this mindset is when Jacqueline saves her brother's life. My wife just got done saving her brother's life. I'm going to tell you about it in 30 seconds.

My wife got a phone call in the middle of the night, and they said, your brother has been jumped in Mexico City at 5 a.m., and somebody beat the hell out of him, and they left him for dead. They dropped him off in front of an old hospital that was barely operating, and literally, the hospital called my wife and said, we want to call you and tell you that your brother will die within the next 12 hours. His brain is swelling. We don't know what to do with him, and he needs to have surgery.

There was no freaking plane flights out until the next morning. My wife calls, gets a private jet, books it out, spends the money, gets to Mexico City, 911. As soon as she gets there, they tell her her brother's going to die within the next 12 hours.

She starts calling all the biggest hospitals and finds all the neurosurgeons. She finds this hospital on the other side of Mexico City and calls this lady who says, "We need to get your brother here now, and we can get him seen." And now it will cost a lot of money, but you must get him here.

So she goes back to the doctor. And she goes, "Hey, I found a hospital to take my brother to. They say they can see him." And the doctor goes, "If you unhook your brother, he's going to die. He's sitting on this bed. He's a vegetable." If you unhook him, which means they have to unhook him, put him in an ambulance, bring him to the other hospital, and hook him back up again, he will die, guaranteed.

My wife literally goes, has a prayer, and says, "I can hear my brother saying, you're going to let me freaking die in this hospital? Get me the heck out of here."

So what does she do? Goes back to the doctor and says, "We've got a private ambulance on the way. We're unhooking him." They go, "All right, you're signing this right now. You just killed your brother. Good freaking job." This is the way they treated her. "You just killed your brother. Good job killing your brother."

Let me tell you something. When you become unstoppable in your life, and you become a person that is obsessed with your goals, you will do anything that it takes. Even when people tell you not to. She unhooks him against the doctor's orders. They take him in an ambulance. They get to the other side and hook him up. Five days later, when he was in a coma, he woke up and looked at my wife and said, "Sister, thank you, sister. You saved my life."

Now, here's the thing. When you make a life or death decision, everybody's going to tell you, "You're going to kill that person." When you make a business or relationship decision, everybody will tell you you will ruin it. It's okay. But you're not always going to make the freaking popular decision. You're going to make the decision based on what is right in your heart. This is about owning your Ownership, taking control, and making the tough calls.

Look, I get it. Integrating your work and family life isn't always easy. It takes effort, communication, and a willingness to adapt. But trust me, the payoff is worth it.

When you have a strong family unit, a partner who's also your biggest supporter, and a life where your work and personal life are aligned, you unlock a level of success and fulfillment that's impossible to achieve any other way.

Remember, you're not just building a business but a life. And that life should be rich, not just financially, but in love, connection, and the unwavering support of the people who matter most.

CHAPTER 4 TAKEAWAYS

- **Honesty is the Foundation:** Open, honest communication is the bedrock of any strong relationship. Embrace those tough conversations.

- **Shared Vision, Shared Victory:** Align on your goals and dreams. Write them down and revisit them often. Let your shared vision fuel your ambition.

- **Teamwork makes the Dream Work:** No one achieves greatness alone. Support each other, celebrate wins, and remember: You and your tribe against the world.

- **Family at the Core:** Make family a priority, involve them, and show them that success is more than money; it's about building a legacy together.

- **Sacrifice with Purpose:** Building an empire requires sacrifice. Make those choices together, ensuring they align with your values and contribute to your greater vision.

- **Love in Action:** Show your love through presence, attention, and unwavering support. Be the rock your family deserves.

You've discovered the essential elements of building an unshakeable family empire: Honesty, Shared Vision, Teamwork, Family at the Core, Sacrifice with Purpose, and Love in Action. Now, apply these principles practically to create a thriving, millionaire marriage. Watch our "How To Become Marriage Millionaires" video at Elliott Training Academy (ETA). Scan the QR code to watch the video and begin building your legacy together.

CHAPTER 5

THE ART OF NOT BLINKING

Before one of my inner circle trainings, when I was in the office, I heard one of my coaches say: "Have you guys noticed that Andy doesn't blink? That's why I want to test you and see if you can't blink the entire time. Leo was like, "I know, I know, Leo, don't you feel like he's just looking at your soul?" That's why his eyes are always red. Me and Jacqueline, we looked at him for a while; we're like, "He doesn't blink, that's why his eyes are always damn red."

Let me tell you something—life is going to hit you. It's going to hit you hard, and it's going to keep hitting. The question is, are you going to blink?

You know me, I'm all about that relentless drive, that unwavering focus. People tell me they see it in my eyes—that "intense Andy focus." They joke about me not blinking. And you know what? They're not far off. Because when you're chasing a vision, when you're building something bigger than yourself, you can't afford to blink.

You can't let doubt creep in. You can't let setbacks derail you. You can't let the world's noise drown out the voice inside you that says, "You got this."

This chapter is about mastering the art of not blinking. It's about developing that unshakeable focus, that relentless determination that will allow you to power through any obstacle and achieve anything you set your mind. It's about tapping into the **WARRIOR** within and channeling that unwavering focus to conquer any battle life throws your way.

There's a reason people say I don't blink. It's not some anatomical quirk or party trick. No, the reason I don't blink is simple: Unwavering focus. Relentless determination. When I lock my eyes on a target, whether closing a sale, building a business, or transforming a life, I don't let anything distract me. I don't flinch. I don't blink.

This isn't something I was born with. Growing up, I was the opposite of focused. I was scattered, undisciplined, always looking for the easy way out. But at 18, when I discovered sales, something changed. I found my calling. And with that calling came a drive, an intensity, a laser focus that would define the rest of my life. It was like activating the "Workout" part of my **WARRIOR**—I was training my mind to be as strong and relentless as my body.

MY STORY:
FROM DOUBT TO DOMINATION

Look, I wasn't born with laser focus. Growing up, I was surrounded by negativity, by people who told me I'd never amount to anything. I had that "failure in my DNA" mentality. I was the kid who barely graduated high school, the one everyone expected to crash and burn. My "Awareness" was clouded by the limitations others placed on me, and I hadn't yet discovered the power to "Recreate" myself.

But something changed when I stepped onto that car lot at 18. I saw a chance to rewrite my story to prove everyone wrong. And I went all in. It was time to take "Ownership" of my life and reach for something bigger.

I became obsessed with mastering the art of selling. I studied the greats, practiced relentlessly, and pushed myself harder than I ever thought possible. I had to make up for lost time, for all those years of doubt and negativity. I was building my "Workout" mentality, pushing myself beyond my perceived limits, and building mental toughness.

And you know what? It worked. I went from being a high school drop-out with nothing to his name to selling 50, 60, even 70 cars a month. I dominated that sales board so hard they had to give me my category!

But it wasn't just about the numbers. It was about proving that I could achieve anything I set my mind to. It was about breaking free from the limitations I had placed on myself and stepping into my full potential. It was about tapping into the "Reach" of my potential and building a legacy that defied expectations.

And that's what I want for you. I want you to experience that same feeling of breaking through, of realizing that you are capable of so much more than you ever thought possible. I want you to unleash your inner **WARRIOR** and claim the life you deserve.

BUILDING YOUR "NOT BLINKING" MUSCLES

So, how do you develop this unwavering focus, this "not blinking" mentality? It's not about becoming a robot devoid of emotion. It's about building mental toughness, about training your mind to stay locked on the target, no matter what life throws your way. It's about cultivating the "Awareness" to recognize distractions and the "Ownership" to shut them down.

Science supports this idea. Neuroplasticity, the brain's ability to change and adapt throughout life, shows our brains are not fixed but can be rewired through experiences, learning, and practice (Doidge, 2007). This means that even if you struggle with focus now, you can train your brain to become more attentive and determined.

Here are a few techniques that have helped me along the way:

FIND YOUR FUEL
What drives you? What gets you fired up in the morning? Is it proving the doubters wrong? Providing for your family? Making a difference in the world? Whatever it is, identify it, write it down, and keep it close. This is your fuel, your motivation to keep pushing when things get tough.

It's about proving those who doubted me wrong and showing others they can achieve anything they set their minds to. It's about breaking those generational curses and building a legacy of success. This is about tapping into the "Reach" of your ambition and using it to fuel your actions.

EMBRACE THE SUCK

Let's be real—achieving anything worthwhile requires hard work, sacrifice, and a whole lot of uncomfortable moments. But here's the thing: you can't let those moments break you. You gotta embrace the suck. You gotta learn to love the grind. Because that's where growth happens, that's where you forge mental toughness. This is where your "Workout" mentality shines—embracing the challenge and pushing through the pain to reach your goals.

Remember when I told you about Jacqueline grabbing my love handle and telling me she and the kids had learned to live without me? Yeah, that was a wake-up call. It sucked to hear, but it lit a fire under me. It forced me to confront my complacency and recommit to my goals. It forced me to "Recreate" myself and become the man I was meant to be.

CONTROL YOUR INPUTS

Your mind is your most powerful tool but is also incredibly susceptible to outside influences. If you're constantly bombarded with negativity, doubt, and fear, that's what will take root in your mind.

You have to be intentional about what you allow into your head. Surround yourself with positive, supportive people. Feed your mind with books, podcasts, and mentors who inspire and challenge you to grow. This is about building a strong "Relationship" with yourself and those who uplift and empower you.

For years now, all I've listened to is leadership and self-development. I've surrounded myself with people who push me to be better. It's like building a mental fortress—the stronger your foundation, the more resilient you become to negativity. This is the power of a strong "Relationship" network—surrounding yourself with those who inspire you to be your best.

FOCUS ON THE DAILY WINS

When you're chasing a big vision, it's easy to get overwhelmed by the sheer magnitude of the task. That's why breaking down your goals into smaller, more manageable steps is crucial. Celebrate those daily wins, no matter how small they may seem.

Remember, success is the sum of small efforts, repeated day in and day out. Each day is an opportunity to improve, strengthen, and get closer to your goals. This ties into the "Workout" mentality—consistent effort over time yields incredible results.

TAP INTO YOUR FAITH

I'm not here to preach, but I'd be lying if I said my faith hasn't played a role in my journey. There have been times when I've faced insurmountable challenges and moments when I felt like giving up. But my faith has always been a source of strength and guidance.

It reminds me that I'm not alone in this; there's a power greater than myself that I can tap into. It gives me that extra push, that unwavering belief that I can overcome anything. This is about tapping into something bigger than yourself, a source of strength and guidance that fuels your "Reach."

But here's the thing: This is about more than just business. The art of not blinking applies to every area of life. It's about setting a goal or vision and pursuing it with determination. It's about blocking out distractions, naysayers, and self-doubt. It's about developing mental toughness and resilience in the face of challenges. It's about becoming the **WARRIOR** you were born to be.

Look at the story of Jacqueline and the house. When told that a house isn't for sale, most people would just move on. But not Jacqueline. She had a vision, a dream, and she wasn't about to blink. She knocked on that door not once but twice. She engaged the owners, made her case, and followed up persistently. And in the end, she made that dream a reality through sheer determination. She tapped into her inner **WARRIOR**, embraced the "Ownership" of her desire, and refused to back down.

That's the power of not blinking. You can achieve the impossible when you refuse to take no for an answer and stay focused on your goal no matter what. You can break through barriers, shatter limitations, and create your desired life. This is the essence of the **WARRIOR** spirit—unwavering determination and a refusal to accept defeat.

Now, I know what some of you are thinking. "That sounds great, Andy, but I'm not like you. I get distracted easily. I lose focus; I give up when things get tough." Trust me, I've been there. Focus and determination aren't innate traits. They're skills, muscles that can be developed and strengthened over time. They are the hallmarks of a true **WARRIOR**, forged through dedication and discipline.

Here are some more techniques that have helped me sharpen my focus and build unwavering determination:

CLARITY OF VISION

The first step is knowing exactly what you want—not a vague idea but a specific, concrete goal you can visualize and describe. Having that clear vision makes it much easier to stay focused. Write it down, make a vision board, or do anything to keep that goal front and center. This is about harnessing the "Awareness" of your desires and using it to guide your actions.

ELIMINATE DISTRACTIONS

We live in a world of constant distractions—notifications, emails, social media, you name it. To develop laser focus, you need to ruthlessly eliminate these distractions. Turn off notifications, block time for focused work, and create an environment conducive to concentration. Treat your focus like a precious resource because it is. This is about taking "Ownership" of your attention and refusing to let distractions derail your progress.

PRACTICE SINGLE-TASKING

Multitasking is a myth. We do everything poorly when we try to do multiple things at once. Instead, practice single-tasking. Give your full attention to one task at a time. When you feel your focus drifting, gently bring it back. Over time, you'll train your brain to sustain focus for longer periods. This is about strengthening your "Workout" mentality, focusing your energy on one task at a time for maximum impact.

DEVELOP RESILIENCE

Focus and determination aren't just about the good times. In fact, they're even more important when things get tough. Resilience is the ability to bounce back from setbacks and to keep pushing forward even when every fiber of your being wants to give up. This is a critical element of the **WARRIOR** spirit—the ability to rise above challenges and emerge stronger.

How do you build resilience? By facing challenges head-on, pushing yourself outside your comfort zone, learning from failures, and using them as fuel for growth. You build that resilience muscle whenever you face adversity and refuse to blink. This is about embracing the "Recreate" pillar, constantly evolving and adapting to overcome obstacles.

HARNESS THE POWER OF HABITS

Habits are the ultimate focus hack. When something becomes a habit, you no longer rely on willpower or motivation; you do it automatically. The key is to build habits that support your goals and your focus.

That means a daily routine of learning, growing and pushing myself. It means surrounding myself with people who challenge and inspire me. It means constantly auditing my habits and eliminating anything that doesn't serve my vision. Over time, these habits have become second nature, and my focus has become unshakeable. This is about aligning your actions with your "Awareness" and creating a system that supports your goals.

LEVERAGE YOUR DRIVE

Ultimate focus comes from knowing what drives you at your core. For me, it's a few key things. I have proven people wrong, broken records, created a brotherhood, and built a legacy for my family. These aren't just nice-to-haves. They're the fire in my belly, so I get up every day ready to conquer the world.

What drives you? Is it providing for your family? Making an impact in your community? Achieving financial freedom? Whatever it is, connect with that drive every single day. Use it as your north star, your unblinking beacon guiding you toward your goals. This is about tapping into the "Reach" of your aspirations and letting it fuel your every action.

THE POWER OF NOT BLINKING

The art of not blinking is about more than achieving success—it's about building a life of purpose, meaning, and impact. It's about becoming the best version of yourself, day in and day out. It's about embodying the warrior spirit and living with unwavering focus and determination.

When you master this skill, you unlock a level of resilience and determination that will allow you to:

- **Power through setbacks:** Obstacles become growth opportunities, and challenges fuel your fire.

- **Silence the doubters:** Their negativity becomes irrelevant as you focus on your vision.

- **Inspire those around you:** Your unwavering belief becomes contagious, motivating others to improve their game.

This is the power of not blinking. It's about living a life of intention, purpose, and unwavering focus. It's about becoming the unstoppable force you were always meant to be. It's about unleashing the **WARRIOR** within and conquering any challenge that stands in your way.

PUTTING IT ALL TOGETHER

Developing unwavering focus and determination isn't a one-time event. It's a daily practice, a constant recommitment to your goals and vision. It's waking up every morning and deciding that today, no matter what comes your way, you will not blink. It's about embracing the **WARRIOR** mentality and showing up as the best version of yourself every single day.

It's simple, but it takes work. There will be days when your focus wavers when your determination falters. That's okay. The art of not blinking isn't about perfection. It's about persistence, resilience, and the willingness to get back up and refocus again and again. It's about embodying the **WARRIOR** spirit, learning from your setbacks, and returning stronger than ever.

As you go through this journey of Total Recreation, keep these principles of focus and determination at the forefront of your mind. Apply the techniques, build the habits, and connect with your drive. Above all, remember that every challenge you face and every obstacle you overcome is an opportunity to strengthen your focus and fortify your determination. Each challenge is a chance to hone your **WARRIOR** spirit and emerge victorious.

You have the power to achieve anything you set your mind to. But it starts with a decision, a commitment to lock your eyes on the prize and not look away. It starts with embracing the art of not blinking. It starts with unleashing the **WARRIOR** within and claiming the life you deserve.

So I ask you again: Are you ready to stop blinking? Are you ready to step into your power and create the life you've always dreamed of? Are you ready to become the **WARRIOR** you were born to be?

The choice is yours.

Set your sights on your vision. Eliminate distractions. Build your resilience. Harness your habits and your drive. And then, with unwavering focus and unshakeable determination, go out and make your dreams a reality. Because that's what Total Recreation is all about. That's the power of living life with your eyes wide open, unblinking and unstoppable. That's the **WARRIOR** way.

CHAPTER 5 TAKEAWAYS

- **Clarity of Vision:** A clear, compelling vision is the foundation of unwavering focus. Know exactly what you want, down to the smallest detail. Write it down, visualize it daily, and let it guide your every action. This is your "Awareness" at work, guiding you towards your goals.

- **Embrace the Suck:** Growth and success lie outside your comfort zone. Embrace the challenges, the discomfort, the "suck." This is where you build mental toughness and resilience. This is where your "Workout" mentality thrives, pushing you to overcome obstacles and emerge stronger.

- **Control Your Inputs:** Your focus is a product of your environment. Surround yourself with positivity, with people and resources that uplift and inspire you. Guard your mind against negativity and distraction. This is about building strong "Relationships" with yourself and those who empower you.

- **Celebrate the Small Wins:** Big goals can be daunting. Break them down into manageable steps and celebrate each small victory. This maintains momentum and motivation. This is about recognizing your progress and fueling your "Workout" mentality with each small win.

- **The Power of Faith:** Faith, whether in yourself, a higher power, or the inevitability of your success, is a potent source of resilience and determination. Cultivate and lean on your faith in times of challenge. This is about tapping into something larger than yourself, a belief that empowers you to "Reach" for your full potential.

- **Habits of Focus:** Unwavering focus is a product of daily habits. Practice single-tasking, eliminate distractions, and regularly engage in 'focus training' to strengthen your concentration muscles. This is about aligning your actions with your "Awareness" and creating a system that supports your goals.

- **Connect to Your Drive:** Lasting determination comes from a deep, intrinsic drive. Connect with your core motivations—the fire in your belly that propels you forward no matter what. Use this as your constant source of inspiration and strength. This is about tapping into the "Reach" of your aspirations and letting it fuel your every action.

These are the keys to developing the art of not blinking and cultivating the unwavering focus and determination that will allow you to achieve anything you set your mind to. But knowledge alone isn't power—applied knowledge and consistent action create real change.

So take these principles and practices and embed them into your daily life. Let them shape your mindset, your habits, and your very identity. When you master the art of not blinking, lock your eyes on your goals, and pursue them with relentless determination, there's no limit to what you can achieve. This is the essence of the warrior spirit—unwavering focus, relentless determination, and an unyielding belief in your ability to achieve anything you set your mind to.

Your journey of Total Recreation continues. Keep your eyes on the prize, stay focused, stay determined, and never blink.

You've learned the key principles of unwavering focus: Clarity of Vision, embracing the suck, controlling your inputs, celebrating small wins, the power of faith, habits of focus, and connecting to your drive. Now, discover how these principles connect to the concept of sacrifice. Watch our video "Sacrifices Are Like Investments" at Elliott Training Academy (ETA). Scan the QR code to watch the video to understand how focused sacrifice can propel you toward your goals and continue your journey.

CHAPTER 6

THE COMPOUND EFFECT OF DAILY GROWTH

Let me tell you something: most people underestimate the power of small, consistent actions. They're looking for the quick fix, the magic pill, the overnight success story. But real, lasting change doesn't happen that way. It's built brick by brick, day after day, through the compound effect of daily growth.

You see, life's a lot like building muscle. You don't walk into the gym once, do a few bicep curls, and walk out looking like Arnold Schwarzenegger. It takes showing up consistently, pushing your limits, and trusting the process. And even then, the results aren't always immediately visible. But I promise you, if you keep at it, the compound effect will kick in, and you'll look back in awe at the transformation.

My life started to change the day I decided to stop being average. But it didn't happen overnight. There was no magic pill, no secret formula handed to me on a silver platter. Recreating myself took years of blood, sweat, and discipline. The key? Focusing on daily growth—stacking small wins daily until they compounded into a massive success.

Most people don't realize that extraordinary results come from actions repeated consistently over time. They want some quantum leap to greatness. But real change is slow and steady. It's embracing the grind with relentless persistence. And that's precisely what I did to transform myself from a scrawny, insecure kid into the beast of the man I am today.

A lot of it came down to my daily routines. I realized early on that if you win the morning, you win the day. And if you win enough days in a row, you win at life. So I became obsessive about my rituals—waking up at 5 am, hitting the gym, listening to self-development, and making sales calls. Day in and day out, I put in the work—even when I didn't feel like it, even when it hurt like hell.

One of my non-negotiables was that I had to sell 3 cars or make 200 cold calls daily. No excuses. I remember dragging myself to the dealership lot, sick as a dog with the flu. Times when I just wanted to quit and go home. But I stuck to the plan. 3 cars or 200 calls every damn day.

And if I didn't hit my sales quota? I punished myself—literally. I'd force myself to run 3 miles as soon as I got home, knowing how much I hated running. My shoes would be waiting for me on the porch, and I'd lace up, even if it was dark or pouring rain. Because I made a promise to myself, and winners always keep their word.

Over time, this kind of discipline became ingrained in me. It was like I rewired my brain for success. The more I pushed myself, the more I could handle it. Discomfort became a compass pointing me toward growth. Slowly but surely, my results started to change.

Every morning, Jacqueline and I do a cold plunge at 5 am. She's not going to let me do anything she's not doing. She's in that bitch with me every morning, just like the dudes. I have to go at least 10 seconds more than her. Here's my point - dudes, chicks, we're all badasses. We're in an era where everyone listening can become a total freaking badass, but I will tell you, it takes discipline and commitment to the daily grind.

Listen, taking care of my fitness helped me build my mental health. Understand this: if your physical health isn't good, your mental health can't be good. It's physically impossible. You want to look at yourself and see a man or woman in the mirror who you're proud of. Proud of how you look, how you answered that phone call, how you interacted with your children. You'll be proud of yourself and everything that you do. That's how you find fulfillment in life - by doing some hard things and feeling powerful because you achieve something great.

My income went up, and my confidence went up. I started stacking accomplishments that seemed impossible before - qualifying for president's club trips, becoming a top salesman, and training leaders on my team. But it all traced back to those daily habits—the ones I never let slide, no matter what.

This is what I mean by the compound effect. It's putting pennies in the bank of success every day until you create real wealth, not just with money but in every area of life - health, relationships, and personal development. This concept is echoed in James Clear's book Atomic Habits, which emphasizes the importance of making small, incremental changes over time. He argues that "success is the product of daily habits, not once-in-a-lifetime transformations" (Clear, 2018). Most people overestimate what they can do in a year but vastly underestimate what they can achieve in 5 or 10 years of consistent effort. That's how you break records and bloodlines.

Now, I know what some of you are thinking. "That's easy for you to say, Andy. You're just built differently. I could never have that kind of drive." And you're right. Not everyone is willing to go to the extremes I did: sleeping on an air mattress, doing two days in the gym, working until your jaw is numb. I get it.

But here's the thing—you don't have to be a maniac to harness the power of micro-improvement. You must raise your standards in a few core areas and commit to the process. Start waking up 30 minutes earlier to pray or meditate. Swap your nightly T.V. binge for a self-help book. Spend the first 15 minutes of your workday making the sales calls you've been putting off.

Building powerful daily routines can be challenging. Life throws curveballs, motivation wanes, and doubt creeps in. That's why having a system, a framework for creating stick routines, is crucial. This is where the **WARRIOR Framework** comes in. It's not just some catchy acronym; it's a battle plan for conquering your day and building a life of unstoppable momentum.

Think about it: a warrior doesn't just wander onto the battlefield hoping for the best. They prepare. They train. They strategize. And that's what the **WARRIOR Framework** is all about - equipping you with the tools and tactics you need to win the war against mediocrity.

One of the most critical pillars of the **WARRIOR Framework** is the Workout. Now, before you skip ahead thinking this is just about hitting the gym, let me explain. Workout is about activating your body and mind for war. It's about pushing your physical limits to build mental toughness and unlock a level of energy and focus most people only dream of.

Remember those 3-mile runs I hated? That was me embracing the Workout mentality. Pushing through the suck, knowing that every step was building the mental fortitude I needed to conquer bigger challenges. And let me tell you, the biological reward is real. Intense workouts release a cocktail of feel-good chemicals in your brain - dopamine, oxytocin, serotonin - that leave you feeling like you can conquer the world.

But Workout is just one piece of the puzzle. The **WARRIOR Framework** is about attacking every area of your life with the same intensity and discipline. It's about developing laser-like Awareness of your strengths, weaknesses, and limiting beliefs. It's about building deep, meaningful relationships with people who will push you to be your best. It's about having the courage to Recreate yourself, shedding old habits and beliefs that no longer serve you.

Integrating every aspect of your life—work, family, personal growth—into a seamless tapestry of purpose and fulfillment. It's about taking radical Ownership of your choices and actions, knowing that you are 100% responsible for the life you create. And it's about using your success to reach beyond yourself, make a difference in the world, and leave a legacy that matters.

The **WARRIOR Framework** is a roadmap to Total Recreation. It's about building a life of strength, purpose, and impact. And the best part is, it all starts with a single decision: to stop being average, to step into the arena of your highest potential, and to commit to the daily grind of becoming the warrior you were born to be.

So, as you forge ahead on your path of daily growth, remember this: you don't have to do it alone. Embrace the **WARRIOR Framework**. Let it guide your steps, fuel your fire, and empower you to create a life that most people wouldn't even dream of.

Let's talk about practicality. How do you actually go about installing these kinds of routines and rituals? It starts with knowing yourself. What do you value most? What are your non-negotiables? What activities fuel you vs.

drain you? The more clarity you have on what matters to you, the easier it is to create aligned habits.

Once you know your core values, it's time to set some standards. Remember, we get what we tolerate. So, if you're tolerating mediocrity in your mornings, that's exactly what you'll attract in your life. Raise the bar for yourself. Make a decision about who you want to be, and then reverse engineer your days to make it happen. Charles Duhigg, in his book The Power of Habit, explains that habits work on a neurological level, forming a loop of cue, routine, and reward (Duhigg, 2012). Understanding this loop allows us to consciously break bad habits and build good ones, creating a foundation for consistent growth.

Here are a few tactics that have worked wonders for me and my team:

- **Bookending:** Lock in a consistent ritual for starting and ending your day, no matter what happens in the messy middle.

- **Habit Stacking:** To make a new habit stick, link it to an existing one. For example, you could tack your new meditation practice onto something you already do religiously.

- **Environment Design:** Shape your surroundings to support your goals. Prep your gym clothes the night before, meal prep on Sundays, and designate device-free zones for deep work.

The most critical factor in creating lasting change is accountability. We all need people in our corner who raise our standards and call us out when we're slipping. That's why I'm such a big believer in brotherhood and mentorship. You need to surround yourself with folks who force you to level up. This is the power of Relationships, another crucial pillar of the **WARRIOR Framework**.

In my company, we have a "no excuses" culture. Everyone knows the standards, and they hold each other to them. If someone misses a workout or skips their calls, you better believe they'll hear about it—not from a place of negativity but out of love and respect because we're all committed to being our best.

Take my coaches, the Macklin twins, for example. These dudes are absolute animals when it comes to work ethic. I've seen them grind for 18 hours straight, totally locked in. And you better believe that rubs off on the rest of us. Their lead-by-example style makes everyone want to push harder. That's the power of proximity. Malcolm Gladwell's research suggests mastering any field requires approximately 10,000 hours of deliberate practice (Gladwell, 2008). While the exact number may vary, the message is clear: consistent effort over time is the key to unlocking your full potential.

But even with all these tools and tactics, the ultimate key to transformation is taking 100% responsibility for your life. Blaming your circumstances, playing the victim, and waiting for someone to save you—that's the old you talking. If you truly want to kill the old you and recreate yourself in the image of success, you've got to step up and own it. This is the essence of Ownership, a non-negotiable in the **WARRIOR Framework.**

That means embracing discomfort, running toward resistance, and facing fear head-on. It means making bold promises to yourself and keeping them, no matter what. It's deciding you're willing to do whatever it takes to have the life you want and backing it up with massive action.

Success is supposed to be hard. If it were easy, everyone would do it. The trials and tests you face on your journey aren't there to break you; they're there to make you unbreakable, to burn away everything that's not essential until only the gold remains.

So, as you forge ahead on your path of daily growth, remember this: every tiny choice matters. Every rep in the gym, every minute of prayer, every phone call, and every night you choose to learn over Netflix shapes you into the person you need to be to live out your destiny. Setting SMART goals— Specific, Measurable, Achievable, Relevant, and Time-bound—is crucial for creating a roadmap for your growth (Doran, 1981). With clear, actionable goals, you can track your progress and celebrate your wins, further fueling your motivation (Amabile & Kramer, 2011).

You've been given a gift, a calling, a mission in this life that only you can fulfill. Don't waste another second doubting your power or settling for less than you're worth. Decide today that you're going to start living from your highest self. That you're going to do the hard things that failures won't. You'll stack so many small wins that they can't help but compound into the extraordinary.

I believe in you. I believe you've got the guts, grit, and resilience to recreate yourself from the inside out. Not because it's easy but because you know the glory of God is within you, urging you onward. You're not just built differently; you're built for more. So let's get after it daily until the whole world notices.

That's the power of Total Recreation. As you become the example of what's possible, you give others permission to do the same. You create a ripple effect of greatness that impacts generations to come. And it all starts with a decision, followed by consistent, courageous action. This is Reach's true meaning, the **WARRIOR Framework's** final pillar.

Let this be your wake-up call, your invitation to step into the arena of your highest potential—not someday, but today, not with perfection, but with persistence. The old you is begging to be shed like old skin. The new you is ready to emerge, forged by the fires of your daily discipline.

All that's left to do is trust the process. When you commit to growth, the universe conspires to support you. Doors will open, mentors will appear, and resources will flow. But you've got to stay the course, especially when it's hard. Embrace the suck and keep showing up. Your future self will thank you.

I'll leave you with this: Success is an inside job, but you don't have to go it alone. Surround yourself with people who see your greatness, even when you can't. Immerse yourself in the wisdom that expands your mind. Lean on your faith and let it fuel you forward. And never, ever forget that every single day is an opportunity to recreate your reality.

It's time to stop being average. Time to kill the old you and birth the legend you were born to become. You've got this. Now, let's go get it, one day at a time. Together, we rise.

CHAPTER 6 TAKEAWAYS

THE COMPOUND EFFECT

- **Incremental Progress:** Lasting change is rarely the result of a single, dramatic action. It's the accumulation of daily choices, the small steps taken consistently over time. Embrace the power of incremental progress, knowing that every positive action is a deposit in the bank of your future success.

- **Non-Negotiables and Consequences:** Define your non-negotiable actions and the daily disciplines essential to your growth. And attach consequences to non-compliance. When you hold yourself accountable and embrace the discomfort of discipline, you build the mental fortitude to overcome any obstacle.

- **Embrace the Suck:** Growth is often uncomfortable. It requires pushing past your perceived limits, facing your fears, and doing the things you don't feel like doing. Embrace the suck, knowing that every challenge is an opportunity to prove your strength and resilience.

You've learned about the power of the Compound Effect, the importance of incremental progress, and the necessity of embracing the suck. Solidify your understanding of building a foundation for lasting change by establishing your non-negotiables. Watch our video "Non Negotiables" at Elliott Training Academy (ETA). Scan the QR code to watch the video to learn how to define, implement, and uphold the daily disciplines that will propel you toward your goals and start compounding your success today.

CHAPTER 7

BUILDING LEADERS, NOT FOLLOWERS

Listen up, because this is where shit gets REAL. Do you want to change your life? Do you want to build something that matters? Do you want to leave a legacy? Then, you have to become a leader. Not just any leader, but a badass MFer who inspires others to rise and become leaders themselves. This is the essence of the Reach pillar—aiming to make a real impact on the world around you.

This isn't some corporate bullshit about delegating tasks and hitting quarterly goals. This is about igniting the fire within you and spreading that flame to everyone you touch. This is about building a brotherhood, an army of unstoppable forces committed to growth, impact, and living a life that most people only dream about. And guess what? That's what building your Relationships is all about - surrounding yourself with a tribe of driven, loyal individuals.

Leadership isn't about titles, positions, or flowcharts. It's about one life influencing another. I never set out to be a leader. I wanted to make a difference, to build something that matters. And in the process, I've discovered that the only way to create lasting change is to empower others to step into their greatness. That's what authentic leadership is all about.

MY PHILOSOPHY:
LEADERS CREATE LEADERS

Let's get one thing straight: leadership isn't a title; it's a responsibility. It's about stepping up, even when you're scared shitless, and saying, "Follow me. I got a plan." It's about believing in yourself so fiercely that it becomes contagious. This unwavering self-belief stems from a deep sense of ownership—taking full responsibility for your actions and their impact.

People are drawn to strength, conviction, and someone who knows where they're going. They can smell bullshit a mile away, but they can also sense authenticity and passion. That's what makes a true leader. And that authenticity? It comes from living in alignment with your core values, a key aspect of the Awareness pillar.

Here's the kicker: real leaders don't hoard power; they empower others. They understand that their success is directly tied to the success of their team, their tribe, and their brotherhood. I believe that we're all born with a seed of greatness inside us. But for most people, that seed stays dormant. It gets buried under fears, excuses, and the expectations of others. As a leader, my job is to help people uncover that seed, nurture it, and give them the tools and belief to grow it.

Bernard Bass's research has shown that transformational leaders, those who inspire and empower their followers, achieve higher levels of performance and satisfaction (Bass, 1985). These leaders create a shared vision, foster a sense of purpose, and unlock the potential within their team members. This aligns perfectly with the idea that leaders create leaders. It's not about controlling or dictating; it's about inspiring and empowering others to reach their full potential.

I judge a leader not by their accomplishments but by the achievements of those they lead. If you want to know if someone's a natural leader, look at the bottom 80% of their team. Are they crushing it? Are they growing? Are they becoming leaders themselves? That's the mark of a true leader. Leadership isn't about creating followers. It's about igniting the leader within each person. It's about challenging people to think bigger, dig deeper, and push past their limits. I'm not interested in creating a bunch of mini-mes running around. I want to build an army of authentic, passionate leaders who will go out and change the world in their unique way.

MORAL AUTHORITY:
THE FOUNDATION OF TRUE LEADERSHIP

But leading a pack of wolves takes more than just charisma and vision. It requires something deeper, something that commands respect and inspires unwavering loyalty. That something is moral authority.

Moral authority isn't about being perfect or preaching from a pulpit. It's about living your values, walking the talk, and being the example you want others to follow. It's about making tough decisions, even when unpopular, and always doing what's right, even when it's hard. This unwavering commitment to your values is a testament to your awareness of who you are and what you stand for.

People can smell hypocrisy a mile away. If you tell your team to work hard while you're slacking off, they'll see right through you. But when you lead with integrity, when your actions align with your words, you earn their respect and trust. You become a magnet for talent, drawing people who want to be a part of something bigger than themselves.

This concept of moral authority is echoed in James MacGregor Burns's work on transformational leadership. He emphasizes the leader's ability to elevate their followers' moral and motivational aspirations (Burns, 1978). This type of leadership fosters a sense of ownership, commitment, and a desire to contribute to something greater than oneself. It's not just about achieving goals; it's about doing so in a way that aligns with a higher purpose and inspires others to do the same.

Think about it. When I was 39, I made a decision to change my life. I was tired of being the guy who talked a big game but didn't always live up to his own standards. I wanted to be an example for my wife, kids, and team. I wanted to be the kind of leader people would follow, not because they had to but because they wanted to. This decision to step up and become a better version of myself required a complete Recreation—shedding old habits and beliefs that no longer served me.

And that's what moral authority does. It creates a gravitational pull, attracting people hungry for growth, purpose, and a leader they can believe in. It's the foundation of a truly unrecruitable team, a team so strong, loyal, and motivated that no one would ever leave, even for more money.

BUILDING YOUR MORAL AUTHORITY: A STEP-BY-STEP GUIDE

So, how do you cultivate this moral authority? It starts with taking a hard look in the mirror and being brutally honest with yourself. Are you living your values? Are you making decisions that align with your beliefs? Are you being the example you want others to follow? This self-reflection is crucial for developing your awareness and identifying areas for growth.

Here are a few actionable steps:

1. **Define Your Values:** What are the principles that guide your life? What do you stand for? Write them down and make them a part of your daily decision-making process.

2. **Walk the Talk:** Don't just talk about your values; live them. Let your actions speak louder than your words. Be the example you want others to follow.

3. **Make Tough Decisions:** Sometimes, the right thing to do isn't the easy thing to do. Be willing to make tough decisions, even unpopular ones, and always stand by your principles. This decisiveness is a hallmark of ownership.

4. **Own Your Mistakes:** We all make mistakes. When you do, admit your mistakes, learn from them, and make amends. This shows humility and builds trust.

5. **Serve Others:** True leadership is about serving something greater than yourself. Look for ways to contribute to your team, your community, and the world around you. This service-oriented mindset is at the heart of the Reach pillar.

Building moral authority is a lifelong journey. It's not about achieving perfection but striving to improve daily. It's about making conscious choices that align with your values and being the kind of leader people are proud to follow.

HOW I BUILT AN ARMY OF LEADERS (AND HOW YOU CAN TOO)

Let me tell you about Elliott Army. It's not just a company; it's a movement. It's a group of underdogs, misfits, and rebels tired of playing small and decided to step into their power. We were all underdogs—misfits, fighters, and dreamers who had faced our share of demons. But we believed in ourselves and each other. We weren't going to settle for average to get by. We made a pact to rise together, to build something legendary.

We have guys like Jacob, who watched his dad get murdered in front of him when he was just a kid. We got Ali, an undefeated MMA fighter who speaks 20 damn languages. These are the people I surround myself with—people who have stared down adversity and come out swinging. This is the power of surrounding yourself with the right Relationships—individuals who uplift and inspire you to reach greater heights.

And you know what? They didn't become leaders overnight. It took hard work, dedication, and a willingness to push themselves beyond their comfort zones. But most importantly, it took a belief in themselves that was ignited by being part of something bigger than themselves. Each had to tap into their inner Warrior, embracing the challenges and pushing their limits to achieve extraordinary results.

Take Jacob. At 24 years old, he had been through more pain than most people face in a lifetime. He was just 10 when he witnessed his father being murdered right in front of him. A tragedy like that can harden people, make them bitter, and close off to the world. But when I met Jacob, I saw a fighter, a young man with an unbreakable spirit. He just needed someone to believe in him and show him his potential.

I took Jacob under my wing and coached him in sales and business. But more than that, I became a big brother to him. I pushed him when he needed tough love and gave him a shoulder when the emotions of his past would resurface. I watched Jacob blossom into a confident, driven young leader. He stopped running from his pain and channeled it into helping others break free from limiting beliefs. Today, Jacob is one of my top lieutenants in the business and a shining example of what's possible when you refuse to let your circumstances define you. Jacob's transformation is a testament to the power of the Recreate pillar—letting go of the past and forging a new, empowering identity.

Every person in my inner circle has a story like Jacob's. Ali, the MMA fighter who never had a real mentor. Ramires, the young immigrant with fire in his belly to build a better life. Amber, the single mom, is determined to give her kids the opportunities she never had. These are the underdog leaders I've bet on, the lives I've gone all in on. Because I know what it's like to be counted out, scraping, and hustling for every inch of success.

But here's the thing—underdogs make the best leaders. We have a chip on our shoulder, something to prove. We're not afraid to get our hands dirty or outwork everyone in the room. When you've been at rock bottom, you develop an unstoppable hunger, a do-whatever-it-takes mentality. And that's exactly what I look for and cultivate in my leaders. This relentless drive is fueled by a deep sense of ownership—taking full responsibility for their lives and outcomes.

My team isn't motivated by titles or corner offices. We're a band of brothers and sisters united by a shared mission to help people live their richest lives. We push each other to be better daily, to look fear in the face, and charge forward anyway. And when one of us succeeds, we all celebrate because we remember the struggle, the late nights and early mornings grinding it out in the trenches together. This shared mission and unwavering support are what make our Relationships so powerful.

That's the kind of bond you can't manufacture. It has to be earned and forged through shared sacrifices and an unwavering commitment to a greater cause. And that bond, that brotherhood, makes us unstoppable as a team. You'll run through walls for each other when you have that depth of trust and loyalty. You become a force of nature, capable of moving mountains and changing the trajectory of lives and industries.

Research backs up the importance of this kind of connection and trust within a team. Google's Project Aristotle, a massive study on team effectiveness, found that psychological safety is the most crucial factor in high-performing teams (Duhigg, 2016). This means creating an environment where team members feel comfortable taking risks, sharing ideas, and expressing vulnerability without fear of judgment or retribution. When people feel safe and supported, they're more likely to contribute their best ideas and work collaboratively towards a common goal.

BUILDING AN UNRECRUITABLE TEAM: ATTRACT AND RETAIN TOP TALENT

Building a team of this caliber isn't about offering the highest salaries or the fanciest perks. It's about creating a culture that people are magnetically drawn to, where they feel valued, supported, and empowered to grow.

Here are a few strategies that have helped me build my unrecruitable team:

1. **Hire for Values:** Skills can be taught, but values are ingrained. Look for people who share your core values and are passionate about your mission. This alignment of values is crucial for building a strong foundation of Relationships.

2. **Invest in Your People:** Show your team that you care about their growth and development by providing training, mentorship, and advancement opportunities. This investment fosters a culture of continuous Recreation and growth. Studies have consistently shown that mentorship positively impacts career advancement, skill development, and overall well-being (Allen et al., 2004). By investing in mentoring programs, organizations can foster leadership development, increase employee engagement, and improve retention rates (Association for Talent Development, 2019).

3. **Create a Culture of Ownership:** Empower your team to take ownership of their work and make decisions. This fosters a sense of responsibility and pride.

4. **Celebrate Successes:** Recognize and celebrate your team's accomplishments, both big and small. This builds morale and reinforces a culture of achievement.

5. **Lead with Love:** Show your team that you care about them as people, not just employees. Be supportive and encouraging, and always have their backs. Leading with love creates a positive and supportive environment where individuals feel valued and respected, strengthening the bonds of Relationships.

When you create a culture like this, you build a team that's more than just a group of individuals working towards a common goal. You build a family, a tribe, a brotherhood united by a shared purpose and an unbreakable bond.

IT'S TIME TO LEAD

Look, the world needs more leaders. People are willing to step up, speak their truth, and inspire others to do the same. You have the potential to be one of those leaders. You have the power to change your life and the lives of those around you.

Remember, leadership is a journey, not a destination. You're never going to "arrive." The key is committing to lifelong learning and always being humble and hungry. Surround yourself with people who will challenge you to keep growing. Seek mentors playing the game at the level you want to attain. This continuous pursuit of growth and self-improvement is fundamental to the Warrior mindset.

Most importantly, always remember your bigger purpose and why you're doing all this in the first place. For me, that reason is to give glory to God, to fulfill the potential He's placed inside me so I can shine a light on others. When my energy fades, and battles get bloody, remembering my "why" keeps me taking the next step. This unwavering commitment to your "why" fuels your Reach and allows you to make a lasting impact.

So whatever your unique reason is, could you keep it in front of you? Let it be the anchor that keeps you grounded and focused. Because here's the deal - leadership can be challenging. If it were, everyone would do it. You'll face doubts, detractors, and moments when you want to throw up your hands and say, "Enough."

But a true leader keeps going long after they feel like quitting. They lead with love even when they're not feeling it. They walk by faith even when they can't see the finish line. Because they know the impact they're capable of making, the lives they have the power to touch. And no temporary pain or problem can compete with that. This resilience and unwavering commitment are hallmarks of the Warrior spirit.

So, leader, it's time to rise up, step fully into your calling, and be the change you wish to see. The world waits for you to embrace your greatness and lead passionately and purposefully. The question is, will you answer the call? Will you do whatever it takes to become the leader you were born to be?

CHAPTER 7 TAKEAWAYS

- **Kill the Follower Mindset:** Real leadership isn't about bossing people around; it's about igniting the leadership potential within everyone you touch. Stop seeking followers and start creating leaders. This embodies the Reach pillar, which aims to create a ripple effect of positive change.

- **Lead Yourself First:** You can't effectively lead others if you're a hot mess yourself. Master your mindset, habits, and actions. Become the person you want others to follow. This self-leadership is a direct reflection of the Ownership pillar.

- **Embrace the Underdog:** Don't underestimate the power of those who have been underestimated their whole lives. Underdogs make the best leaders because they're hungry, driven, and never back down from a challenge. They embody the Warrior spirit—resilient, determined, and always ready to fight for what they believe in.

- **Build a Brotherhood (or Sisterhood):** True leadership is built on trust, loyalty, and a shared mission. Create a culture where people feel valued, supported, and empowered to rise together. This is the essence of powerful Relationships.

- **It's Not About You:** Servant leadership is the only kind that lasts. Focus on adding value to others, helping them achieve their goals, and empowering them to become the best versions of themselves. This selfless approach aligns with the Reach pillar—positively impacting the world.

- **Remember Your Why:** Leadership is a marathon, not a sprint. There will be tough times, setbacks, and moments when you want to quit. But when you're connected to a purpose bigger than yourself, you'll find the strength to keep going. Your "why" is the driving force behind your Reach and your commitment to making a difference.

You've explored the core principles of effective leadership: killing the follower mindset, leading yourself first, embracing the underdog, building a brotherhood/sisterhood, focusing on others, and remembering your why. Now, delve deeper into leadership dynamics and learn how to avoid common pitfalls that can cause you to lose your people. Watch the "Why Leaders Lose Their People" video at Elliott Training Academy (ETA). Scan the QR code to watch the video and strengthen your leadership skills.

CHAPTER 8

THE POWER OF BROTHERHOOD

Brothers, let me tell you something. No one - and I mean no one - makes it to the top alone. You might think you're the baddest alpha on the planet, that you've got what it takes to conquer the world solo. But let me set you straight right now. That's a fool's game. The path to true greatness, breaking blood-lines and shattering limits, is paved with brotherhood. It's about building your tribe—your band of brothers—who will be there for you through thick and thin, push you to be your best and celebrate your victories like their own.

When I started, I thought I could do it all myself. I hustled nonstop, grinding day and night, pushing myself to the brink. But no matter how hard I worked, something was missing. It wasn't until I started surrounding myself with a loyal inner circle, a true band of brothers, that things started to click. We were united by a shared vision—to build an empire that would change the game. And that's what we did, brick by freakin' brick.

Let me paint a picture for you. It's the early days of my company, and we're operating out of this tiny office space. The walls are bare, and the furniture's secondhand, but none matters. Every day, my team shows up ready to run through brick walls. We're knocking down walls, painting, drywalling—doing whatever it takes to build our empire. And yeah, we could've hired some fancy contractors to do it for us. But that's not the point.

The point is that we were building something together. Brick by brick, wall by wall, we poured our blood, sweat, and tears into a shared vision. Those long nights and backbreaking days forged an unbreakable bond between us. Now, when one of my guys sees a chair out of place, they push it in. When there's trash on the floor, they pick it up—not because they have to but because they're part of something bigger than themselves. That's the power of brotherhood. Extensive research has shown that social support plays a crucial role in buffering the negative effects of stress and promoting both physical and mental health. Individuals with strong social support networks tend to have lower levels of stress hormones, stronger immune systems, and reduced risk of chronic diseases (Cohen & Wills, 1985).

I remember this one time I was going through a rough patch. Betrayal, business struggles, you name it. I was ready to throw in the towel, tell everyone to screw themselves. But then I saw my guys, my inner circle, standing strong. They didn't judge me, didn't offer empty platitudes. They just listened, offered support, and reminded me who the hell I was. They were my rock, and they helped me weather that storm. Social support is also a key factor in building resilience and enhancing coping abilities in the face of adversity (Southwick, Bonanno, Masten, Panter-Brick, & Yehuda, 2014). Individuals who feel supported by others are better equipped to navigate challenges, overcome setbacks, and bounce back from difficult experiences.

That's the power of brotherhood, right there. It's about having people who believe in you even when you don't believe in yourself. People who call you out on your bullshit and challenge you to step up your game. People who celebrate your victories like their own and pick you up when you fall.

And let me tell you, building a brotherhood like that ain't always easy. It takes time, effort, and a whole lot of intentionality. But trust me, it's worth every damn ounce of energy you pour into it.

Think about it like building an unrecruitable army. You need warriors who are in it to win it, who share your values, and who are willing to fight for something bigger than themselves. That kind of brotherhood will conquer any challenge and achieve the impossible.

So, how do you build this kind of brotherhood? Let me break it down for you:

1. **Surround Yourself with Truth-Tellers:** The first step, is to surround yourself with people who tell you the truth, even when it's hard to hear. You don't need yes-men or people who are afraid to call you out on your crap. You need people who love you enough to tell you when you're screwing up, who challenge your perspectives, and who push you to grow. Remember, iron sharpens iron. You want to be around people who make you uncomfortable, who force you to level up and become a better version of yourself. They're not good friends if they give you the answer you want. They're not good friends if they're telling you what you want to hear. If they're challenging you and telling you, "Hey, well, what did you do to piss her off?" That might be a good friend. You know, somebody that's going to challenge you, somebody that's going to tell you the truth is what you need to hear.

2. **Seek Out Loyalty and Trust:** Loyalty and trust are the cornerstones of any true brotherhood. You need to know that the people you're running with have your back, no matter what. And they need to know the same about you. Look, I've been burned before, betrayed by people I thought I could trust. It hurts like hell. But you know what? It taught me the importance of surrounding myself with people who are ride or die and who have proven their loyalty time and time again. I remember Dana White. Whenever Joe Rogan was getting canceled, Dana White would say, "Joe Rogan was there for me before anybody else was. I was nobody, and Joe Rogan was becoming somebody. And then when they were canceling Joe Rogan, Dana White would say, 'You cancel him, you cancel me.'" That's loyalty. That's brotherhood.

3. **Find Your Tribe, Your Pack:** We're not meant to do life alone. We're wired for connection, for community. That's why it's so important to find your tribe, your pack—a group of like-minded individuals who share your values, support your dreams, and push you to be your best. For me, that's my team at The Elliott Group. We're more than just colleagues. We're a family. We work, play, and have each other's backs, no matter what. And you know what? We get insane results because of it. We're breaking records, building a movement, and changing lives. And it's all because we're united, aligned, and committed to a common goal. As humans, we have a fundamental need to belong (Maslow, 1943). When we feel connected to a group, whether it's a brotherhood, a team, or a community, we experience a sense of purpose, motivation, and a willingness to contribute to something greater than ourselves (Tajfel & Turner, 1979).

4. **Embrace Vulnerability and Honesty:** Real brotherhood requires vulnerability. It's about being open and honest with each other, even

when it's scary. It's about sharing your struggles, fears, and dreams and knowing you won't be judged. I'm not saying you must spill your guts to everyone you meet. But you need to have a few trusted individuals with whom you can be 100% authentic, who you can let your guard down around, and who can just be yourself.

5. **Be There for Each Other, No Matter What:** True brotherhood is a two-way street. It's about being there for each other through thick and thin. It's about celebrating the victories together and supporting each other through the tough times. When one of us is down, we rally around them, offering encouragement, support, and whatever resources they need to get back on their feet. That's what brothers do. We lift each other up.

CREATING A CULTURE OF UNWAVERING LOYALTY

Building a brotherhood is about more than just finding a group of guys to hang out with. It's about creating a culture of unwavering loyalty, where each member feels a deep sense of belonging and purpose. This requires a conscious effort to foster an environment encouraging growth, vulnerability, and mutual support.

Think about it like this: you're not just assembling a team but creating a brotherhood of warriors. And every warrior needs a code, a set of shared values and principles that guide their actions and bind them together.

Here are some actionable steps you can take to cultivate this kind of culture within your brotherhood:

- **Establish Shared Values and Goals:** What core principles bind your brotherhood together? What are you collectively striving to achieve? Define these values and goals explicitly and ensure everyone is on the same page. This is about creating a shared identity, a sense of purpose that transcends individual ambitions.

- **Foster Open and Honest Communication:** Encourage a culture of transparency and open dialogue. Create a safe space for members to share their struggles, fears, and dreams without judgment. Remember, the real strength lies in vulnerability. When you can be open and honest with each other, you build trust and create an environment where everyone feels safe to be themselves. Google's

Project Aristotle revealed that psychological safety is the most important factor in high-performing teams (Duhigg, 2016). When team members feel safe to take risks, share ideas, and be vulnerable, they can tap into their collective intelligence and achieve extraordinary results (Woolley et al., 2010).

- **Celebrate Victories Together:** When one member achieves a win, celebrate it as a collective victory. This reinforces the sense of shared purpose and strengthens the bond between members. Remember, success is sweeter when it's shared.

- **Provide Unwavering Support During Challenges:** When a brother faces a tough time, rally around him and offer unwavering support. This could be through emotional encouragement, practical assistance, or simply being a listening ear. True brotherhood is forged in the fires of adversity. When one of you falls, the others pick him up, dust him off, and remind him of his strength.

- **Invest in Each Other's Growth:** Encourage members to invest in personal and professional development. Create opportunities for learning, mentorship, and accountability. Remember, iron sharpens iron. When you challenge each other to grow, you all become stronger.

- **Foster a Sense of Belonging:** Ensure every member feels valued and appreciated. Create rituals and traditions that reinforce the sense of community and belonging. This could be as simple as having regular team dinners, celebrating birthdays, or creating a tradition unique to your brotherhood.

By implementing these strategies, you'll create a brotherhood that's more than just a group of friends. You'll build a powerful force for good, a team of individuals committed to each other's success and positively impacting the world.

Listen, building a brotherhood takes work. It's not always easy. But I'm telling you, it's worth it. Having that kind of support system, that kind of bond with other men, it's a game-changer. It will change your life. I guarantee it.

Now, some of you might be going through hell right now. I get it, believe me. Life can be a cruel bitch sometimes. One day, you're on top of the world; the next, you're face down in the dirt, wondering what happened. But I need you to hear this. Those moments, those trials by fire, they're not a sign that God's abandoned you. They're a sign that the devil's noticed you, that he sees your value. And he'll do anything to isolate you, to pull you away from your pack.

Don't let him. Lean into your brotherhood; lean into the people who've been there since day one. My team and coaches are ready to go to war for you at a moment's notice. All you have to do is reach out. Don't try to weather the storm alone; don't buy into the lie that you're better off solo.

Stay connected, stay hungry, stay in the freaking pack. Because that's where the growth happens, you'll find the strength to keep pushing, even when every fiber of your being is telling you to quit. And trust me, if you stay the course and keep showing up with that psycho-competitor mindset, there's no limit to what you can achieve.

So dream bigger, brothers. Dream so freaking big it scares you. Then, go out and find the people who will fight like hell to make that dream a reality. Build your army, your brotherhood, and then conquer the world.

Because, at the end of the day, that's what this is all about. It's about living a rich-ass life in your bank account and soul. It's about waking up every morning excited to tear into the day, about going to bed at night knowing you left it all on the field. And most importantly, it's about doing it together.

So let's freaking go. Let's show the world what true brotherhood looks like and what alpha energy can achieve. Let's build our empires brick by brick, shoulder to shoulder, until we're so damn high they'll need a space shuttle to reach us.

The journey won't be easy, but nothing worth having ever is. There will be blood and sweat; there will be times when you want to throw in the towel. But if you've got your brothers by your side and that unshakeable bond of loyalty and love, then there's no challenge too great, no obstacle too high.

So look to your left, look to your right. Those are your brothers, your ride-or-die. Cherish, challenge, and push them to be better than they ever thought possible. And most importantly, never let them walk alone. Because, in the end, that's what brotherhood is all about. It's about having someone to lean on when the world's beating you down, about having someone to celebrate with when you reach the mountaintop.

And if you can master that and harness the true power of brotherhood, then I promise you, there's no limit to what you can achieve. You'll break bloodlines, shatter generational curses, and build a legacy that will echo through eternity. So let's get to work, brothers. Let's show the world what we're made of and do it together because that's the only way to live a life worth living - with our brothers by our side, ready to run through hell and come out the other side even stronger. Let's freaking go.

Alright, we've covered a lot of ground in this chapter. I've shared stories about the early days of building this company, our sacrifices, and the unbreakable bonds we forged through shared hardship and vision. I've discussed the importance of surrounding yourself with the right people, loyalty, and having each other's backs. But I don't want these to be stories. Please take these principles and these lessons and apply them to your own life. So, let's break it down; let's distill the essence of harnessing the power of brotherhood.

CHAPTER 8 TAKEAWAYS

- **Shared Experiences Build Unbreakable Bonds:** Remember building that empire brick by brick? That's what I'm talking about. There's something powerful about going through hardship together, about working towards a common goal. Those shared experiences—the late nights, the setbacks, the triumphs—create a bond that can't be broken. Seek out those opportunities to build, struggle, and win together.

- **Surround Yourself with Your Unrecruitable Army:** You don't need yes-men. You need warriors, truth-tellers who will challenge you to be your best, even when uncomfortable. Surround yourself with people who believe in you, support you, and push you to grow.

- **Loyalty Above All:** Loyalty is everything. When someone has been there for you, when they've had your back through thick and thin, you honor that. You show that same loyalty in return. No matter what. Build a team of ride-or-die loyalists, and be that same loyal teammate in return.

- **Fight for Resolution, Not Victory:** Conflicts will happen. It's inevitable. However, we should approach those conflicts to find a solution that works for everyone, not just win the argument. Be willing to have the hard conversations, to work through the discomfort, in service of greater harmony.

- **Stay Connected to Your Pack:** Isolation is the enemy. You're most vulnerable when you feel yourself pulling away and tempted to retreat into your struggles. Stay connected to your team and your brotherhood. Let them be your strength when you're feeling weak.

- **Embrace the Struggle:** If you're going through hell, keep going. Adversity is not a sign of failure; it's a sign that you're on the path to something great. The enemy only attacks what's valuable. So if you're getting your ass kicked, congratulations - you're a threat. Keep pushing.

Brotherhood, a shared mission, and a commitment to loyalty and growth are the pillars of an unstoppable team. In your business, family, or personal relationships, seek opportunities to forge unbreakable bonds. We need each other because life is too short and hard to go alone. We need that ride-or-die crew that will stand with us through anything.

So go out and build your brotherhood. Find your team. Create a culture of loyalty, hard conversations, struggle, and triumph. And watch as you all rise together to heights you never could have reached alone.

You've learned the importance of shared experiences, surrounding yourself with the right people, prioritizing loyalty, fighting for resolution, staying connected, and embracing the struggle. Now, dive deeper into building and maintaining a truly exceptional team. Watch our video "Leadership Training - Recruiting and Retaining a Savage Team" at Elliott Training Academy (ETA). Scan the QR code to watch the video and discover how to create an unbreakable bond with your team.

CHAPTER 9

DOMINATING IN SALES

Let's cut to the chase. You want to dominate in sales. You want to crush it, obliterate your competition, and build a life of abundance. I get it. I've been there. From selling 70-80 cars a month when the average was 8 to building a nine-figure business, I've learned a thing or two about what it takes to win in this game. And let me tell you, it's not about some magic formula or secret handshake. It's about mindset, strategy, and relentless execution—unleashing your inner **WARRIOR**.

This chapter is about giving you the tools and the no-BS truth to transform yourself into a sales powerhouse. We'll dive into the mindset shifts that will unlock your true potential, the battle-tested strategies that have made me millions, and the real-world examples from my career that will show you what's possible when you commit to becoming a sales master.

Are you ready to get your mind right and start crushing it? Let's go.

If there's one area of life where you must kill the old you, it's in sales. The average doesn't cut it here. You're either dominating or you're losing. There's no in-between.

I learned this lesson early on in my career. By the time I was 20, I was selling 50-60 cars a month at the dealership. My numbers were so high that the managers didn't even want to put me on the sales board because it demoralized the rest of the team. Everyone else was selling 8 or 10, but I was doing 50, 60, even 70-80 as I got into my 20s.

You see, I had a relentless drive to be successful and annihilate the competition. I wasn't content with simply being number one. I wanted to be in a league of my own, on my own damn island. That's the level of dominance you need to aim for in sales - the **WARRIOR** mentality.

But how do you get there? It starts with your mindset. You must develop an unshakable belief in achieving the seemingly impossible. You have to be delusional in your pursuit of greatness. And you have to be willing to outwork, out-hustle, and out-care everyone else. You must train your mind like a **WARRIOR** trains for battle, relentlessly pushing past your limits and embracing the grind.

IT STARTS IN THE MIND:
THE SALESMAN'S CREED

Before getting into the tactics and techniques, we need to address the foundation—your mindset. The truth is, sales is a game won and lost in the mind. You can have the best product, the smoothest pitch, but if your head isn't screwed on right, you're going to get crushed.

Here are the non-negotiable mindset shifts that will separate you from the pack:

- **Psycho-Competitor Mentality:** This isn't about being a jerk; it's about having an unquenchable thirst to be the best. You need to crave the win more than you fear the loss. You must be willing to outwork, outlearn, and out-hustle everyone else in the room. Remember, the average guy sold 8 cars; I sold 80. Why? Because I was obsessed with being the best. This is the **WARRIOR** spirit in action, the relentless pursuit of excellence.

- **Ownership Mentality:** Whether you're running your own business or working for someone else, you must treat every sale like your own company. Take extreme ownership of your results, your relationships, and your growth. When you act like an owner, you think differently, you act differently, and you get different results. This is about stepping onto the battlefield of sales as the commander of your own destiny, just like a true **WARRIOR**.

- **Unwavering Belief:** If you don't believe in your product or service, neither will your customer. You need to cultivate unwavering conviction in the value you provide. This isn't about hype or BS; it's about knowing in your core that your offer can change lives. When you have that level of belief, it radiates outwards and becomes infectious. This is the **WARRIOR'S** unwavering faith in their cause, the unshakeable belief that drives them forward.

- **Embrace Discomfort:** The world is trying to get comfortable, but comfort is the enemy of growth. The more uncomfortable you get, the more addicted you'll become to doing hard things. Embrace the challenges, the setbacks, the rejections. They are the fire that forges your resilience and builds your character. This is the **WARRIOR'S** willingness to face their fears, to step into the arena and fight even when it's uncomfortable.

Remember, your mindset is the foundation upon which everything else is built. Cultivate these mental shifts, and you'll be well on your way to dominating sales.

MASTERING A STRANGER:
TURNING INTERACTIONS INTO OPPORTUNITIES

Now, let's discuss a crucial skill that can make or break your success in sales: the art of mastering a stranger. This is about more than just making a good first impression. It's about quickly building rapport, establishing trust, and creating a connection that leads to a sale and a long-term relationship. It's about recognizing humanity in every interaction and approaching each encounter with the respect and dignity of a warrior.

Here are some techniques I've used to turn strangers into clients and friends:

- **Focus on the Person, Not the Product:** People can smell a sales pitch a mile away. Instead of leading with your product or service, focus on getting to know the person in front of you. Ask questions, listen actively, and show genuine interest in their needs and challenges. Remember, every person you meet is fighting their own battles. Approach them with empathy and understanding, like a

WARRIOR extending a hand of camaraderie. Research by Neil Rackham, author of SPIN Selling, emphasizes the importance of asking insightful questions to understand customer needs and challenges (Rackham, 1988). Salespeople who focus on uncovering customer needs and tailoring their solutions accordingly are more likely to close deals and build long-term relationships.

- **Find Common Ground:** Look for shared interests, experiences, or values that can create a connection. This could be anything from a favorite sports team to a passion for a particular cause. Common ground builds bridges and fosters trust, essential qualities in the **WARRIOR'S** arsenal.

- **Be Authentic and Vulnerable:** People are drawn to authenticity. Don't be afraid to let your guard down, share your own story, and be vulnerable. This creates a sense of trust and makes you more relatable. Vulnerability is not weakness; it's strength. It's the **WARRIOR** showing their humanity, connecting on a deeper level. The Harvard Business Review emphasizes the importance of active listening in building rapport and trust with customers (Levine, 2016). Salespeople who demonstrate a genuine interest in their customers' concerns and perspectives are likelier to create a positive and productive sales experience.

- **Practice Active Listening:** Pay attention to what the other person is saying verbally and nonverbally. Ask clarifying questions, summarize their points, and show that you're truly engaged in the conversation. Active listening is a sign of respect, a **WARRIOR'S** way of honoring the person in front of them.

- **Offer Value Upfront:** Don't wait for the close to start providing value. Share a helpful tip, offer a free resource, or go above and beyond to make their experience positive. Generosity is a hallmark of a true **WARRIOR**, demonstrating their commitment to service and building lasting relationships. One of Robert Cialdini's six principles of persuasion is reciprocity, which suggests that people feel obligated to return favors and acts of kindness (Cialdini, 2007). By offering value upfront, you trigger this principle and increase the likelihood of a positive response.

Mastering a stranger is a skill that takes practice. But the more you do it, the more confident and effective you'll become. And the more opportunities you'll create to build relationships, close deals, and make a real impact.

FROM THE TRENCHES:
BATTLE-TESTED SALES STRATEGIES

Now that we've got your mind right and you're ready to connect with anyone let's talk about the strategies that will turn you into a sales machine. These are the tactics I've used to close deals, build empires, and change lives. They are the battle-tested strategies of a warrior, honed through experience and forged in the fires of real-world challenges.

- **Set Non-Negotiables:** You need to have a system, a set of non-negotiables that hold you accountable and drive consistent action. For me, it was the 3-car, 200-call, 3-mile rule. If I didn't sell 3 cars, I had to make 200 calls. If I missed both, I had to run 3 miles. Find what works for you, write it down, and stick to it like your life depends on it. The **WARRIOR'S** code is their unwavering commitment to discipline and action.

- **Master the Art of Communication:** Sales is all about communication, but it's not just about talking; it's about connecting. You must learn to build rapport, ask the right questions, listen actively, and influence emotions. Remember, people buy from people they like and trust. A true **WARRIOR** is a master communicator, able to inspire, motivate, and persuade with integrity and authenticity.

- **Provide Massive Value Upfront:** One of the best ways to stand out is to give away your best stuff for free. That's right, I said free. When I first started my sales training company, I created YouTube videos that were better than my competitor's paid courses, and I gave them away for free. This built a massive following, established me as an authority, and ultimately led to more sales than I could have imagined. Generosity is a powerful weapon in the **WARRIOR'S** arsenal, disarming the competition and building trust with potential allies.

- **Focus on Transformation, Not Transactions:** Don't just sell a product or service; sell a solution, a transformation. People are looking for more than just a quick fix; they want to improve their lives. When you focus on the impact you can have on your customer's life, the sale becomes about something much bigger than just a transaction. A true **WARRIOR** doesn't just fight for themselves; they fight for a cause, for a better future. Prospect theory, developed by Daniel Kahneman and Amos Tversky, highlights the concept of loss aversion, which suggests that people are more motivated to avoid losses than to acquire gains (Kahneman & Tversky, 1979). Framing your sales message regarding the potential losses your customer faces by not investing in your product or service can be a powerful way to highlight the transformative value you offer.

- **Build Raving Fans:** Your goal shouldn't be to close a sale but to create a raving fan. Raving fans are your best customers, brand ambassadors, and walking, talking testimonials. Go above and beyond for your customers, over-deliver your promises, and build lasting relationships. A warrior knows the value of loyalty and builds a tribe of supporters who will stand by them through thick and thin. Salesforce, a leading CRM provider, reports that companies using CRM systems experience significant increases in sales revenue and customer retention rates (Salesforce, 2023). CRM systems provide valuable insights into customer behavior, allowing businesses to personalize their communications and tailor their offerings to meet specific needs (Gartner, 2023). Building raving fans is about leveraging the power of relationships and utilizing tools like CRM to enhance your customer connection.

Remember, these strategies are only as good as your execution. Commit to mastering these skills, and you'll be on your way to crushing your sales goals.

WALKING THE TALK: REAL-WORLD EXAMPLES

You might think, "Andy, this all sounds great, but does it work?" Let me give you a few real-world examples from my career that will show you the power of these principles in action. These stories are not just anecdotes; they are battle scars and testaments to the power of the **WARRIOR** spirit to overcome adversity and achieve extraordinary results.

FROM $5 TO $1,700 COMMISSION ON DAY ONE
When I was 18 years old, I walked into my first sales job with no experience, no money, and a bit of a stutter. That day, I made a $1,700 commission. How? I embraced the training, applied what I learned, and went after it with everything I had. It was my first taste of victory, a sign that I had the heart of a **WARRIOR**.

BEATING GRANT CARDONE WITH FREE YOUTUBE VIDEOS
When I decided to enter the automotive sales training market, I was up against some stiff competition, including Grant Cardone. Instead of trying to outspend him, I outworked him. I created hundreds of free YouTube videos that provided more value than his paid training. This strategy allowed me to dominate the market and taught me the power of generosity and building a loyal following. It was a David vs. Goliath story, a testament to the **WARRIOR'S** ability to outsmart and outmaneuver the competition.

JACQUELINE'S "WINNERS GET AN ROI" LESSON

One day, I felt down about a training program I had invested in. I was ready to give up and ask for a refund. My wife, Jacqueline, looked at me and said, "Winners get an ROI regardless of the training program." That one sentence changed my entire perspective. I realized my success was ultimately up to me, not the program. I doubled down on my efforts, extracted every ounce of value I could, and ultimately achieved the results I was looking for. It was a reminder that the **WARRIOR'S** journey is not always easy, but the unwavering belief in oneself ultimately leads to victory.

These are just a few examples of how the principles and strategies we've discussed can lead to real-world success. Remember, your story is still being written. What kind of legacy are you going to create? What battles will you win? What victories will you achieve? It's time to step into the arena and claim your destiny as a **WARRIOR.**

THE SPIRITUAL SIDE OF SALES

I know what you might think: "Andy, you've been talking about mindset, strategies, and tactics, but what about the spiritual side?" Listen, I'm a man of faith, and I believe God has played a massive role in my success. But here's the thing: God helps those who help themselves.

You can pray for sales all day, but nothing will happen if you're unwilling to work, develop the skills, and change your mindset. Faith without works is dead. You must be willing to step out in faith, take action, and trust that God will meet you halfway.

Remember, success is not about luck but preparation for meeting opportunities. The magic happens when you align your actions with your faith and combine your hard work with God's grace.

But here's the thing: when you operate at this level and genuinely dominate, it's not just about the money. It's about the person you become, the lives you impact, and the difference you make.

I truly believe that God has blessed me with a gift for sales, not just for my own benefit, but so that I can be a blessing to others. The real magic happens when you approach your work with that mindset and focus on genuinely helping people.

So here's my challenge to you: raise your standards in sales. Set audacious goals for yourself and then pursue them relentlessly. Develop a delusional belief in your own potential. Outwork everyone. Out-care everyone. Build real relationships. And never, ever settle for average.

That old version of you that was content with mediocrity? That version that hid from discomfort and shied away from the phone? That version that cared more about their own commission than their customers' well-being? It's time to kill that version. It's time to step into the dominator you were always meant to be. It's time to unleash your inner **WARRIOR**.

Will it be easy? Heck no. Will there be days that you want to quit? Absolutely. But mental toughness continues even when you don't feel like it. When the alarm goes off and you don't want to make those calls, you do it anyway. Day after day, you show up as your best self. You empty the tank every single day.

That's the path to sales greatness. There are no shortcuts, no quick fixes. It's simple, but it ain't easy. It's waking up every day and consciously choosing to be a hunter. Choosing to be relentless. Choosing to raise the freaking bar for yourself and never look back. It's about embracing the **WARRIOR** spirit and living a life of purpose, passion, and unwavering commitment.

DOMINATE YOUR DESTINY

Look, I didn't write this chapter to fill pages. I wrote it to ignite a fire in your belly. I want to show you that dominating in sales and life is a choice. It's about embracing the grind, pushing past your limits, and becoming the person you were destined to be. It's about unleashing the **WARRIOR** within and conquering the world on your own terms.

Remember, the world is full of people who are content with average. Don't be one of them. Embrace the psycho competitor within, commit to relentless execution, and watch as you achieve levels of success you never thought possible. This is your call to arms, an invitation to join the elite ranks to become a sales **WARRIOR**.

I'll tell you this: on the other side of that, hard work is a life beyond your wildest dreams. When you truly dominate sales, you create freedom for yourself and your family. You create impact. You create a legacy. And you get to live life on your own terms. This is the reward of the **WARRIOR**, the spoils of a life lived on the offensive, a life of victory and triumph.

So let me ask you: are you ready to kill the old salesperson inside you? Are you ready to take your game to the next level? Are you willing to do whatever it takes to become the best version of yourself?

If so, it's time to embrace the grind. It's time to go all in. It's time to start dominating every single day. Your next level of life is waiting for you. And it all starts with a decision. Decide to become a sales master. Decide to kill average. Decide to live a life with no regrets. Decide to become a **WARRIOR**.

You've got this. It's time to unleash the sales beast inside you. It's time to show the world what you're really made of. Let's freaking go.

Now, go out there and dominate.

CHAPTER 9 TAKEAWAYS

- **Unleash Your Inner WARRIOR:** Dominating in sales requires a warrior mentality—relentless drive, unwavering belief, and a willingness to embrace discomfort.

- **Mindset is King:** To unlock your sales potential, cultivate a psycho-competitor mindset, take extreme ownership, believe in your product, and find comfort in discomfort.

- **Master the Art of Connection:** Turn strangers into clients by focusing on them, finding common ground, being authentic, actively listening, and offering upfront value.

- **Embrace Battle-Tested Strategies:** Implement proven tactics like setting non-negotiables, mastering communication, providing massive value, focusing on transformation, and building raving fans.

- **Walk the Talk:** Real-world examples demonstrate the power of these principles—embrace challenges, learn from setbacks, and celebrate victories.

- **Align Your Spirit:** Combine hard work with faith, approach sales with a spirit of service, and use your success to make a difference.

- **Take Action:** Apply the personal and business exercises to transform your mindset, habits, and sales approach.

- **Dominate Your Destiny:** Commit to the journey, push past your limits, and become the sales **WARRIOR** you were born to be.

You've discovered the key principles of dominating in sales: unleashing your inner WARRIOR, mastering your mindset, connecting with clients, embracing proven strategies, leading by example, aligning your spirit, and taking action. Now, deepen your understanding of the sales WARRIOR mindset and how it can unlock your full potential. Watch our video "Sales Training - Develop This Mindset & You Can Have It All" at Elliott Training Academy (ETA). Scan the QR code to watch the video and transform your sales approach.

CHAPTER 10

THE ART OF NURTURING RELATIONSHIPS

Let's talk about relationships! Not just the romantic kind, though those are crucial too. I'm talking about the entire network of humans you surround yourself with - your family, friends, mentors, business partners, clients, and even the barista who makes your morning coffee. These connections, my friend, are the most valuable currency you'll ever possess. They are the foundation of a rich-ass life, the fuel that propels you towards your wildest dreams. This, my friends, is the **WARRIOR** way.

You might be thinking, "Andy, I'm a lone wolf. I don't need anyone. I can achieve greatness on my own." And while I admire your ambition, let me tell you something: that's a load of bull. Even the most successful people in the world didn't get there alone. They had a team, a support system, a tribe of badasses who had their back and pushed them to be better. Just like a **WARRIOR** needs their unrecruitable army, you need your people.

Think about it: who's going to celebrate your wins with you? Who will pick you up when you fall flat on your face (because, trust me, you will)? Who will challenge you to grow and become the best version of yourself? It sure as hell ain't gonna be your Instagram followers. You need genuine connections with people who believe in you, even when you don't believe in yourself. Research has shown time and time again that strong social connections are one of the most significant predictors of happiness and well-being (Lyubomirsky, 2008). The Harvard Study of Adult Development, which followed hundreds of men for over 80 years, found that close relationships are the key to a happy and fulfilling life. The study suggests that people prioritizing their relationships with family, friends, and community tend to be healthier, happier, and live longer (Vaillant, 2012).

In the world of business and personal growth, there's one critical factor that can make or break your success: relationships. Building, maintaining, and leveraging strong relationships is a superpower that can open doors, create opportunities, and propel you to new heights. But here's the thing—most people don't have a system for nurturing their relationships. They wing it, hoping the occasional text or phone call will suffice. But to achieve massive success, you must intentionally cultivate your connections. You need to build your own personal **WARRIOR** network.

That's where the concept of a personal CRM comes in. CRM stands for Customer Relationship Management, a tool businesses use to track and manage their interactions with clients and prospects. But why limit this powerful concept to just business? Personal relationships are just as important, if not more so, than professional ones. By creating a personal CRM, you can ensure that you're consistently nurturing the relationships that matter most to you.

Now, I know what some of you might be thinking. "Andy, I don't have time for all that. I have a business to run, a family to care for, and a life to live." Trust me, I get it. But here's the thing—the time you invest in your relationships is never wasted. In fact, it's one of the best investments you can make. When you prioritize your relationships, you create a powerful network of supporters, advisors, and collaborators who can help you achieve your goals and navigate life's challenges. This is about Integration, bringing all aspects of your life together to create a force multiplier for success.

THE SCOTTSDALE SHIFT: HOW CHANGING MY ENVIRONMENT TRANSFORMED MY BUSINESS

I've always been a big believer in taking massive action. So, when Jacqueline and I decided to uproot our lives and move to Scottsdale, Arizona, we didn't hesitate. We sold our house, packed our bags, and went all-in on this new adventure. And let me tell you, it was the best damn decision we ever made. We took Ownership of our environment and Recreated our reality.

Scottsdale wasn't some magical utopia where success fell from the sky. We still had to grind, hustle, and put in the work. But the environment, energy, and people we surrounded ourselves were game-changers.

See, in Oklahoma, we were comfortable. We had a good life and a nice house, but there was this nagging feeling that something was missing. We were surrounded by people who were content with the status quo, and that energy was contagious. It was slowly sucking the life out of our dreams. Our Awareness of this stagnation was crucial to breaking free.

Scottsdale, on the other hand, was a breeding ground for ambition. Everyone was on a mission to level up their lives; that energy was infectious. We were surrounded by entrepreneurs, innovators, and high-performers playing the game at a different level. And being around that kind of energy, it lit a fire under our asses.

We started connecting with like-minded individuals, building genuine relationships with people just as hungry for success as we were. We found mentors who had walked our path and were willing to share their wisdom. Most importantly, we created a support system that held us accountable and pushed us to improve daily. We were building our warrior tribe.

The move to Scottsdale wasn't just about changing our physical location, mindset, network, and entire life approach. It was about surrounding our-selves with people who elevate, challenge, and support us on our journey to greatness.

When we arrived in Scottsdale, we started building relationships with the people around us. We joined local business groups, attended networking events, and conversed with anyone who crossed our path. And you know what? People responded. They were drawn to our energy, authenticity, and willingness to connect deeply.

One of the key relationships we formed was with a successful entrepreneur, my brother Brad Lea. Brad had built a multimillion-dollar business from scratch and had a wealth of knowledge and experience to share. But more than that, Brad had a heart for helping others succeed. He took us under his wing, introduced us to his network, and provided invaluable guidance as we navigated this new chapter.

Our business exploded through Brad and the other relationships we cultivated in Scottsdale. We landed new clients, formed strategic partnerships, and expanded our offerings in ways we never imagined. But more than that, we found a community of people who shared our values and vision for positively impacting the world.

Not everyone can move to a new city like we did. However, the principle remains the same—the relationships you surround yourself with profoundly impact your success and happiness. Think about it this way—networking is not just about collecting business cards; it's about building genuine connections and cultivating relationships that provide support, opportunities, and new perspectives (Granovetter, 1973). LinkedIn's research consistently shows that professionals who actively network are more likely to find jobs, advance in their careers, and earn higher salaries (LinkedIn, 2023).

As I mentioned before, "Loyalty is very rare. Trust, trust is the big one." Building trust and loyalty in your relationships is essential for long-term success. And it's not just about what you can get from others but also what you can give. "If you don't care for your people, someone else will. This is a rule that I learned in life." The principle of reciprocity, as described by Robert Cialdini, suggests that people are more likely to help those who have helped them (Cialdini, 2007). By being generous with your time, knowledge, and resources, you can build stronger relationships and create a positive cycle of reciprocity (Hyde, 2007). This is about building your **WARRIOR** tribe, a group of people you trust implicitly who have your back no matter what.

YOUR PERSONAL CRM:
BUILDING A NETWORK THAT FUELS YOUR SUCCESS

Listen up because this is important. Most people focus on building a CRM (Customer Relationship Management) for their business, which is great. But what about your personal life? Do you have a system for nurturing the relationships that matter most?

Just like you nurture leads in your business, you need to nurture the connections in your personal life. These people will be there for you through thick and thin, celebrate your victories, and help you navigate the inevitable challenges that life throws your way. They are your personal board of advisors, support system, and **WARRIOR** council.

So, how do you build a killer personal CRM? Here are a few tips:

1. **Identify Your Tribe:** Take a hard look at the people you spend the most time with. Are they lifting you up or dragging you down? Are they aligned with your values and goals? Surround yourself with people who inspire, challenge, and make you want to be a better version of yourself. This is about building your **WARRIOR** network, a group of people who will push you to be your best.

2. **Be Intentional with Your Time:** Time is your most valuable asset, so invest wisely. Schedule a regular time for coffee dates, phone calls, or even quick text messages with the people who matter most. Remember, relationships are like plants; they must be watered and nurtured to thrive.

3. **Be Present and Engaged:** Be fully present when you're with someone. Put your phone away, listen attentively, and engage in meaningful conversations. People can tell when you're not really there, and it shows a lack of respect for their time and energy.

4. **Give More Than You Take:** The strongest relationships are built on reciprocity. Don't just focus on what you can get from others; look for ways to add value to their lives. Offer support, share your knowledge, and be there for them when they need it most. I always say, "Relationships are the most valuable currency you can have. How is it that you can always over-deliver?"

5. **Don't Be Afraid to Be Vulnerable:** Authenticity is magnetic. People are drawn to those willing to be open and vulnerable, to share their struggles and triumphs. Letting your guard down and allowing others to see the real you create a deeper connection and trust.

6. **Seek Out Mentors:** Find people a few steps ahead of you on the path you want to take and learn from their experiences. Mentors can provide invaluable guidance, support, and accountability as you navigate the ups and downs of life.

7. **Pray for guidance:** I'm not here to preach, but I firmly believe in the power of prayer. When you're struggling to find your tribe or build strong relationships, ask God for guidance. He'll put the right people in your life at the right time.

Building a solid network takes time and effort, but the rewards are immeasurable. These connections will enrich your life in countless ways, providing support, inspiration, and opportunities for growth that you wouldn't have access to otherwise. So, get out there, start building those relationships, and watch your life transform.

I want to be clear: nurturing relationships takes effort, time, energy, and intentionality. But the payoff is immeasurable. When you have a strong network of supporters, advisors, and collaborators, you have a powerful force for good in your life. You have people who will challenge you to grow, pick you up when you fall, and celebrate your successes as if they were their own.

And here's the beautiful thing—by nurturing your relationships, you enrich your life and create positivity that touches everyone around you. You become a beacon of light in a dark and disconnected world. You show others what it means to live a life of purpose, passion, and connection.

So, my challenge to you is this: start intentionally nurturing your relationships today. Create your personal CRM, reach out to someone you've been meaning to connect with, and look for ways to add value to the people in your life. And as you do, remember that you're not just building a network—you're building a legacy—a legacy of love, service, and impact that will live on long after you're gone.

And one more thing—don't forget to thank God for the people He's placed in your life. Every relationship is a gift, a chance to learn, grow, and love more deeply. By honoring those gifts and using them to make a difference in the world, you'll fulfill your highest calling and live a life that truly matters.

So go out there and start nurturing those relationships. You've got this. And remember - you're never alone on this journey. You've got a community of supporters, a loving God, and a fire inside you that can never be extinguished. Let's go change the world, one relationship at a time.

RECLAIMING YOUR POWER: TAKEAWAYS AND EXERCISES FOR TOTAL RELATIONSHIP DOMINATION

We've explored the incredible power of relationships and how they shape our lives, businesses, and identities. We've seen how surrounding ourselves with the right people can ignite our ambition, challenge us to grow, and support us through life's inevitable ups and downs. Now, let's summarize the key takeaways from this chapter and the guiding principles that will help you nurture the most important relationships.

CHAPTER 10 TAKEAWAYS

- **Your Network is Your Net Worth:** The relationships you cultivate are your most valuable currency ever. Invest in them wisely, and they will pay dividends for a lifetime.

- **Be Intentional:** Building strong relationships doesn't happen by accident. Proactively seek and nurture connections with people who inspire, challenge, and share your values.

- **Create Your Personal CRM:** Like businesses manage customer relationships, you need a system for nurturing personal connections. Identify your tribe, schedule regular touchpoints, and always look for ways to add value.

- **Embrace Vulnerability:** Authenticity is the foundation of deep, meaningful relationships. Don't be afraid to let your guard down, share your struggles, and allow others to see the real you.

- **Seek Out Mentors:** Find people who have walked the path you want to follow and learn from their wisdom. A good mentor can accelerate your growth and help you avoid costly mistakes.

- **Give More Than You Take:** The best relationships are built on a foundation of generosity. Look for ways to contribute to others' lives through your time, knowledge, or resources.

- **Pray for Guidance:** When struggling to build your desired relationships, turn to God for guidance. Trust that He will bring the right people into your life at the right time.

When applied consistently, these principles have the power to transform your life and your business. By nurturing your relationships with intention, authenticity, and generosity, you'll create a powerful network of support that will help you weather any storm and achieve your wildest dreams. So start today—reach out to someone you admire, schedule that coffee date, and build relationships that will enrich your life for years.

You've learned the key principles of building a powerful network: understanding your network's worth, being intentional, creating a personal CRM, embracing vulnerability, seeking mentors, giving more than you take, and praying for guidance. Now, implement these principles and learn how to cultivate deeper, more meaningful connections. Watch our "Let The Other Guys Quit" video at Elliott Training Academy (ETA). Scan the QR code to watch the video and maximize your net worth today.

CHAPTER 11

KILLING THE OLD YOU

Let's get real for a second. You picked up this book because something's gotta change. You're tired of the same old routine, the same old results, the same old you staring back in the mirror. You know there's more to life, a whole other level you're destined to reach. But something's holding you back. That something? It's the old you.

Killing the old you isn't about becoming someone you're not. It's about shedding the layers of fear, doubt, and limiting beliefs that have kept you stuck. It's about confronting the comfortable mediocrity that's become your existence and saying, "Enough is enough!"

Total Recreation is about taking a sledgehammer to your comfort zone and rebuilding your life from the ground up. It's about rewriting your story, redefining your limits, and stepping into the most powerful, authentic version of yourself. This transformation requires tapping into your inner **WARRIOR**, unleashing the power within to conquer your limitations and achieve true greatness.

And let me tell you, it's the most exhilarating, terrifying, and rewarding journey you'll ever embark on.

There comes a point in every person's life when they must decide - do I continue down the path of mediocrity, or do I burn it all down and recreate myself from the ashes? This is the essence of Total Recreation, the complete annihilation of your old identity to make space for the person you were meant to become. It's a process that requires guts, grit, and an unshakable belief in your own potential. But let me tell you, it's worth every ounce of blood, sweat, and tears. It's about embracing the **WARRIOR** within, who refuses to settle for anything less than extraordinary.

My journey of total Recreation began when I was at my lowest point. I was broke, stuck in a dead-end job, and drowning in self-doubt. I looked in the mirror and saw a man I didn't recognize, a shell of the person I once dreamed of becoming. That's when I heard a voice whisper, "Andy, it's time to kill the old you." It was a call to activate my inner **WARRIOR**, to rise above the challenges and become the man I was destined to be.

At first, I resisted. The old me was comfortable and familiar. I wasn't happy, but at least I knew what to expect. Deep down, I knew I was meant for more. I couldn't shake the feeling that there was a greater purpose for my life, a calling I had ignored for far too long. My inner warrior was dormant, yearning to break free.

So, I made the decision to change. I committed to doing whatever it took to transform my life, even if it meant facing my deepest fears and insecurities. I knew it wouldn't be easy, but I also knew that the price of staying the same was far greater than the pain of growth. This was my call to arms, my initiation into the **WARRIOR'S** path.

Look, I get it. Change is scary. Trust me, I've been there. For years, I was living a lie. On the outside, I was crushing it. I was making serious money selling cars, and I had the big house, the fancy cars, and the whole nine yards. But inside? I was empty. My inner **WARRIOR** was trapped, starved for purpose and authenticity.

I was a slave to my job, constantly chasing the next commission check. I wasn't present for my wife, Jacqueline, or my kids. I was just going through the motions, existing instead of truly living. I had neglected the "Relationships" and "Integration" pillars of the **WARRIOR Framework**, sacrificing my personal life for the illusion of success.

I remember Jacqueline and I were preparing for a rare night out one evening. I struggled to button my pants, my gut hanging over the waistband. Jacqueline, knows how to light a fire under my backside. She looked at me, grabbed my love handle, and said, "You're getting comfortable." She knew I had stopped pushing myself and stopped striving for more. My inner **WARRIOR** was getting soft.

That one sentence, it sent shivers down my spine. It was like a bucket of ice water had been thrown on me. She was right. I had become complacent, settling for a life that was a fraction of what I could. I had lost sight of the "Workout" pillar, neglecting my physical health and, in turn, my mental sharpness.

Jacqueline warned me. This is a warning to all of you. She warned me that I was not living up to my potential. I could either go down the ego road and fight against her or look in the mirror and say, 'I'm a winner on my own' and get better. And I made a decision to change. I had to kill my ego to listen to Jacqueline. Some of you right now are very hard to coach because your ego, pride, and entitlement are standing in the way. Ego is the death of you. I need you to be open-minded. Write that down, and be open-minded that there's a different way, a better way. And expect it to be complicated. If only you could do the hard things, why would you even think it would be easy? I'd instead tell you the truth. It's going to be the hardest freaking thing you've ever done in your whole life. You've got to embrace the "Ownership" pillar, take responsibility for your shortcomings, and commit to becoming the best version of yourself.

That night, I went into our garage and stared at myself in the mirror. I saw a guy who was lost, a guy who had settled for mediocrity, a guy who had betrayed himself. I made a decision right then and there. I was done with the old Andy. It was time to unleash the **WARRIOR** within.

The first step in my Total Recreation was identifying the limiting beliefs and behaviors holding me back. I had to be honest with myself about how I was sabotaging my own success. For me, it was a lack of self-confidence, a fear of failure, and a tendency to procrastinate when things got tough. This is where "Awareness" comes in, the crucial self-reflection that allows you to identify and confront your weaknesses.

I realized that these patterns were deeply ingrained and passed down through generations of my family. It was like I was carrying the weight of my ancestors' mistakes on my shoulders, doomed to repeat their cycles of poverty and dysfunction. But I refused to let my past define my future. I made a conscious choice to break the bloodline, to shatter the generational curses that had been holding me back. This is about rewriting your story, taking control of your destiny, and forging a new path for yourself and future generations.

This meant surrounding myself with people who challenged me to improve and believed in my potential even when I didn't believe in myself. I sought mentors and coaches who had already achieved the success I aspired to and studied their habits and mindsets. I devoured books and courses on personal development, soaking up knowledge like a sponge. This is the power of Relationships: surrounding yourself with a tribe that lifts you higher, pushes you further, and helps you become the warrior you were meant to be.

But knowledge alone wasn't enough. I had to take massive action to practice my new beliefs daily. This meant pushing myself out of my comfort zone, taking risks, and embracing failure as a necessary part of growth. This is where the rubber meets the road, where you work, embrace the grind, and transform yourself into a force to be reckoned with.

I started hitting the gym hard. I shaved my head, a symbolic act of shedding the old me. I started reading everything I could to get my hands on self-development, devouring the wisdom of guys like Tony Robbins and my brother Andy Frisella, who taught me the importance of setting high standards.

But the biggest change? It was internal. I committed to myself, Jacqueline, and my kids to become the man I was always meant to be. This is about aligning your actions with your values, integrating your personal and professional life, and living purposefully.

It was challenging. We sold our house, got rid of almost everything we owned, and moved into a tiny rental. I quit my high-paying job to pursue my dream of building a sales training company. People thought I was crazy. They said I was throwing away everything I had worked for.

But you know what? I had never been more sure of anything in my life. I was tired of living a lie. I was done with mediocrity. I was ready for my Total Recreation. I was ready to embrace the **WARRIOR'S** path, no matter the cost.

And let me tell you, the journey has been wild. We've faced challenges I never could have imagined. Sometimes, I wanted to give up, crawl back into my comfort zone, and pretend none of this ever happened.

Honestly, there's a point that some of you, if you want to go as big as me and Jacqueline want to go in building a nine-figure business as quick as we did, there are some days that honestly, we felt like we were going to be hospitalized, exhausted. When you hear that, you're like, oh my God, that sounds awful. We didn't want to get rich when we had a dream bigger than ourselves. Me and Jacqueline wanted to kill off our old life so bad. Since we messed up 15 years and wasted them, we wanted to figure out how to ensure we never wasted another minute.

So now that we were cramming things that people would do in a month, we were doing it in a day. We were running so hard, and we still do. And by the way, I want to tell you something. This is a secret. You build the strength to endure more as you go. It's like this. You get addicted to it. And you get addicted.

But I didn't give up. I kept pushing, kept growing, kept believing in myself and the vision I had for my life. And you know what? It paid off.

Today, I'm living a life beyond my wildest dreams. We have a thriving business, a beautiful home, and, more importantly, I have an incredible relationship with my wife and kids. I'm finally living a life of purpose, passion, and fulfillment.

It all started with the decision to kill the old me by embracing the warrior within.

Now, it's your turn. Are you ready to shed the old you and step into your power? Here's how to get started:

1. **Make the Decision:** This is the first and most crucial step. With every fiber of your being, you must decide you're done with the old you. Write down what you're no longer willing to tolerate in your life. What are you ready to leave behind? This is your declaration of war against mediocrity, your commitment to becoming a **WARRIOR**.

2. **Embrace Discomfort:** Growth happens outside your comfort zone. Challenge yourself daily. Set audacious goals that scare you. Embrace the suck, knowing that on the other side of discomfort lies incredible transformation. This is where you forge your **WARRIOR**

spirit, pushing past your limits and embracing the challenges that make you stronger.

3. **Find Your Tribe:** You can't do this alone. Surround yourself with people who support your growth, challenge you to improve, and hold you accountable for your goals. Find your brotherhood, your tribe of like-minded individuals who will push you to become the best version of yourself. This is your "Relationships" pillar in action, building a network of support that will empower you on your journey.

4. **Develop a Growth Mindset:** Research by Carol Dweck has shown that individuals who believe their abilities can be developed through effort, learning, and persistence (what she calls a "growth mindset") tend to achieve higher levels of success and are more resilient in the face of challenges (Dweck, 2006). Embrace challenges as opportunities for growth. View setbacks as lessons, not failures. Cultivate an insatiable thirst for knowledge and a willingness to learn and adapt. This is about constantly seeking improvement, upgrading your skills, and mastering your craft.

5. **Take Action:** Don't just talk about it, be about it. Take consistent action towards your goals, even if it's just one small step each day. Remember, the compound effect is real. Small, consistent actions over time lead to massive results. This is where "Ownership" comes into play, taking responsibility for your progress and making things happen.

6. **Prioritize Your Health:** Your physical and mental health are paramount. Fuel your body with nutritious foods, exercise regularly, and prioritize sleep. When you feel your best, you perform your best. This is the "Workout" pillar, the foundation of your **WARRIOR** physique and mindset.

7. **Live a Life of Service:** True fulfillment comes from positively impacting the world. Find a cause you're passionate about and dedicate your time and energy to making a difference. This is about embracing the "Reach" pillar, using your success to uplift others and leave a legacy that matters.

8. **Trust the Process:** Transformation takes time. Be patient with yourself and celebrate your progress along the way. Trust that you are exactly where you should be. This is about having faith in your journey and knowing that the challenges and setbacks are all part of the plan.

9. **Never Stop Growing:** Total Recreation is a lifelong journey, not a destination. Commit to continuous learning, growth, and self-improvement. Embrace the unknown and never stop pushing yourself

to become the best version of yourself. This is the essence of the **WARRIOR** spirit, the relentless pursuit of excellence in all areas of life.

As you embark on your journey of Total Recreation, know you are not alone. Lean into the support of your tribe and trust that you have a plan for your life greater than anything you could imagine.

And remember, Total Recreation is not about becoming someone else. It's about becoming more fully yourself, the version of you you were created to be. It's about stripping away the masks and the facades and stepping into your authentic truth. It's about unleashing the **WARRIOR** within.

So, take a deep breath and take the first step. Kill the old you and give birth to the new. Embrace the process of Total Recreation, and watch as your life transforms before your very eyes. Because on the other side of death is rebirth, and on the other side of fear is freedom. You were made for this. You were made for more.

Now go out there and recreate your damn life. I'll be cheering you on every step of the way.

CHAPTER 11 TAKEAWAYS

- **The Decision to Recreate is Yours:** Total Recreation starts with a decision, a moment of clarity when you say, "Enough is enough." It's a commitment to yourself, a promise to leave mediocrity behind and embrace your true potential as a **WARRIOR**. Make that decision today, and never look back.

- **Embrace discomfort as a Catalyst for Growth:** Growth lives outside your comfort zone. Embrace the challenges, setbacks, and moments of doubt and fear. These are the catalysts for your transformation, the fire that forges your strength and resilience as a warrior.

- **Break the Bloodline of Limitation:** We all carry the weight of our past, the limiting beliefs and behaviors passed down through generations. But you have the power to break the cycle, to shatter the generational curses that have held you back. Refuse to let your history define your destiny. Become the **WARRIOR** who breaks free and creates a new legacy.

- **Surround Yourself with Your Warrior Tribe:** You are the average of the five people you spend the most time with. Surround yourself with mentors, coaches, and peers who challenge you to be better and believe in your potential even when you don't believe in yourself. Their wisdom and support will be invaluable on your journey.

- **Massive Action Fuels Transformation:** Knowledge without action is just potential. You must take massive, consistent action toward your goals to recreate yourself. Embrace failure as a necessary part of the process, and keep pushing forward no matter what. This is the warrior spirit in action.

- **Transformation is Holistic - Integrate Your WARRIOR Within:** Total Recreation is about changing your external circumstances and transforming from the inside out. Prioritize your physical, mental, and spiritual health, and cultivate a growth mindset that embraces challenges as opportunities. Cognitive Behavioral Therapy (CBT) can be a powerful tool in this process, helping you identify and change negative thought patterns and behaviors that hold you back (Hofmann et al., 2012). By focusing on your present-moment thoughts and actions, you can gain control over your mind and create positive changes in your life (Beck, 1976).

- **Your Purpose is Bigger than You - Reach for Greatness:** True fulfillment comes from positively impacting the world. As you recreate yourself, seek ways to serve others and use your gifts and talents for the greater good. When you align your personal growth with a higher purpose, you tap into a well of unimaginable strength and resilience.

Remember, killing the old you is not a one-time event; it's a lifelong commitment to growth and self-discovery. Embrace the journey, trust the process, and never stop striving to become the best version of yourself. The world needs your light, your unique gifts and talents. So step into your power, and let your Total Recreation be a beacon of hope and inspiration for all those who follow in your footsteps.

You've identified the core principles of Total Recreation: making the decision to change, embracing discomfort, breaking the bloodline of limitation, surrounding yourself with a supportive tribe, taking massive action, integrating your WARRIOR within, and reaching for a purpose bigger than yourself. Now, put these principles into action. Watch our video "Skills" at Elliott Training Academy (ETA). Scan the QR code to watch the video and begin your transformation today.

LIVING A RICH-ASS LIFE

Let's get real for a second. What does it really mean to live a "rich-ass life"?

You see it plastered everywhere—on social media, in movies, even in the breakroom at work. People chase money, fame, and possessions, thinking that's the ticket to the good life. But let me tell you something, having walked that path and come out the other side: It's not about the Benjamins filling your bank account. It's about something much deeper that money can't buy but can only amplify.

It's about building a life where every aspect—your relationships, purpose, health, and impact on the world—is firing on all cylinders. It's about becoming the best version of yourself, the person you were always meant to be, and living with a fire in your belly that can't be extinguished. Total Recreation is completely renovating your mind, body, and spirit.

Jacqueline and I have been through the wringer. We've sacrificed, hustled, stared down failure, and become stronger on the other side. And you know what we learned? True wealth is the kind that makes you sleep well at night and look in the mirror with pride; that's not about the digits in your bank account. It's about the richness you cultivate in every area of your life. It's about embodying the **WARRIOR** within.

Remember back in the day when I told you about selling everything we had and driving beat-up cars? People thought we were crazy. But we were chasing a dream, a vision of a life we could be proud of. We were willing to risk it all, look stupid, and start from scratch because we knew that true wealth wasn't about holding onto material possessions but the courage to chase our vision. We were activating our inner **WARRIOR**, embracing the "Workout" and "Reach" pillars without realizing it.

And that's the first lesson I want to hammer home: Don't be afraid to sacrifice. Comfort is the enemy of progress. If you want an extraordinary life, you have to be willing to make extraordinary sacrifices. That might mean giving up some luxuries, working long hours, or walking away from relationships that no longer serve you. It won't be easy, but the rewards are worth it. Remember, a **WARRIOR** doesn't shy away from discomfort; they lean into it, knowing it forges their strength.

Just look at my friend Greg. He had it all—the high-paying job, the fancy house, the luxury car. But he was miserable. He was working 80-hour weeks, missing his kids' soccer games, and barely speaking to his wife. One day, he decided enough was enough. He quit his job, downsized his lifestyle, and started his own business doing something he loved. It was scary as hell, and sometimes, he didn't know how to pay the bills. But you know what? He persevered, and now he's living life on his own terms. He's present for his family, passionate about his work, and has never been happier. Greg chose to "Recreate" his life, embracing the unknown and building something true to himself.

Now, let's talk about fear. We all have it: fear of failure, fear of judgment, fear of the unknown. But here's the thing about fear: it's a liar. It will keep you trapped in mediocrity, whisper doubts in your ear, and hold you back from your true potential. A true **WARRIOR** recognizes fear for what it is—an illusion, a phantom to be vanquished.

Do you want to know the secret to overcoming fear? Action. Massive, relentless action. The more you act despite fear, the weaker its grip on you becomes. Remember when I told you about facing my fears head-on, even when my heart was pounding in my chest? That's how you break free from fear's grip—you step into the arena, even when terrified, and fight for the life you deserve. You tap into the "Ownership" pillar, taking control and refusing to be ruled by fear.

I'll always remember the first time I spoke on stage. I was shaking like a leaf, my palms were sweating, and I thought I was going to puke right there in front of everyone. But I took a deep breath, reminded myself why I was there, and approached the mic. And you know what? It wasn't perfect, but I survived. And the next time was a little easier, and the time after that was even easier still. Now, speaking on stage is one of my favorite things to do. I've learned to channel that fear into fuel, to let it propel me forward instead of holding me back. I "Recreated" my relationship with fear, turning it from an enemy into a source of power.

Speaking of fighting, let's discuss another crucial element of a rich-ass life: building a strong foundation. For me, that foundation is rooted in my faith, my family, and my team. These are the people who have my back no matter what, who believe in my vision, and who push me to be better every single day. This is the "Relationships" pillar of the **WARRIOR Framework**—the unwavering support system that allows you to conquer any challenge.

Surround yourself with people who lift you higher, who challenge you to grow, and who celebrate your victories alongside you. Remember what I said about the power of the pack? You can achieve anything when you have a loyal team by your side, a team built on trust, respect, and a shared vision.

I think about my friend Sarah. For years, she struggled with her weight and her self-confidence. She tried every diet under the sun, but nothing seemed to stick. It wasn't until she found a community of like-minded women, all working towards the same goal of health and wellness, that things started to click. They lifted each other up, held each other accountable, and celebrated every milestone. Sarah was able to lose weight with their support, but more importantly, she gained a newfound sense of self-love and self-respect. She built her "tribe," her support network, and it transformed her life.

You might be thinking, "Andy, this all sounds great, but how do I create this 'rich-ass life' you're talking about? How do I activate my inner warrior and start living with purpose?"

I'm glad you asked. Here's the deal: it starts with you. It starts with a deep-down, unshakeable decision that you're done with average and ready to step into your power and create an extraordinary life. It starts with

"Awareness"—a deep understanding of who you are, what you want, and what's holding you back.

One crucial aspect of a rich-ass life that often gets overlooked is financial well-being. I'm not talking about chasing millions or becoming obsessed with money. I'm talking about having a healthy relationship with money, understanding how it works, and using it as a tool to create the life you want. This is where financial literacy comes in.

The National Financial Educators Council (NFEC) reports that individuals with higher financial literacy are more likely to make informed financial decisions, save for retirement, manage debt effectively, and achieve financial goals (NFEC, 2023). Financial literacy is not just about having money; it's about knowing how to manage it, invest it, and make it work for you.

The Consumer Financial Protection Bureau (CFPB) emphasizes the importance of financial education in reducing financial stress and improving overall well-being (CFPB, 2023). Stress about money impacts every area of life—your relationships, your health, and your peace of mind. But when you have a solid understanding of your finances and a plan for the future, it frees you up to focus on the things that truly matter.

Once you've decided to take control of your finances, it's time to work on designing a life that lights you up. I'm not talking about clocking in and out of a job you hate. I'm discussing designing a life aligned with your values, passions, and purpose. It's about "Recreating" your reality and forging a unique path that aligns with your definition of a "rich-ass life."

This is where the principles of positive psychology come into play. Martin Seligman, a pioneer of positive psychology, proposed the PERMA model, which outlines five key elements of well-being: Positive emotions, Engagement, Relationships, Meaning, and Accomplishment (Seligman, 2011).

Think about it. When you're engaged in work that you're passionate about, have strong, supportive relationships, feel a sense of meaning and purpose in your life, and achieve your goals—that's when you're truly living a rich-ass life.

And here's another key ingredient: giving back. Research has shown that helping others can benefit those in need and enhance our happiness and well-being (Post, 2007). The Greater Good Science Center at UC Berkeley has found that altruistic acts can trigger a release of endorphins, reduce stress, and improve mood (Greater Good Science Center, 2023).

When you focus on making a difference in the world, on using your gifts and talents to serve others, you experience a level of fulfillment that money can't buy. It's about tapping into the "Reach" pillar of the **WARRIOR Framework**—extending your impact beyond yourself and leaving a legacy that matters.

Here are a few exercises to get you started on your journey to a rich-ass life:

1. **Define Your "Rich-Ass Life" Vision:** Grab a notebook or open up a fresh Google Doc, and let's get clear on what a truly fulfilling life looks like for you. Don't hold back. Write down everything you desire—your relationships, finances, health, and impact on the world. What does your dream life look and feel like? This is about tapping into the "Reach" pillar—envisioning the legacy you want to leave behind.

2. **Identify Your Fears and Limiting Beliefs:** Now, let's get real about the things holding you back. What fears are whispering doubts in your ear? What limiting beliefs are keeping you stuck? Write them down, shine a light on them, and then ask yourself, "Are these thoughts serving me? Are they true?" This exercise is about cultivating "Awareness," shining a light on the shadows that hold you back.

3. **Create Your "Burn the Boats" List:** This is about crystalizing the things you're willing to let go of to create space for your desired life. What habits, beliefs, or even relationships are no longer serving you? Write them down, and then, literally or metaphorically, burn that list. It's time to release the dead weight and step into your power. This is "Recreation" in its purest form—shedding the old to make way for the new.

4. **Develop Your "Action Plan" for Total Recreation:** Now that you have a clear vision for your "rich-ass life" and you've identified the obstacles in your way, it's time to create a plan of attack. Break down your goals into smaller, actionable steps. What can you do today, this week, and this month to move closer to your vision? This is where "Ownership" comes into play—taking responsibility for turning your vision into reality.

5. **Cultivate an Attitude of Gratitude:** This is huge. When you focus on the good in your life and appreciate your blessings, you open yourself up to receiving even more abundance. Start a gratitude journal, express your appreciation to those you love, and make it a habit

to find joy in the little things. Gratitude is a powerful force that amplifies the positive in your life, strengthening your "Relationships" and attracting even more abundance.

So, let me wrap this up with a final thought. Living a "rich-ass life" isn't about perfection. It's about more than figuring it out or never facing challenges. It's about living with intention, purpose, and a relentless commitment to growth. It's about surrounding yourself with people who bring out the best in you and being that same kind of person for others. It's about savoring the journey, even the messy parts, and knowing that each step brings you closer to the life you were meant to live. It's about embodying the **WARRIOR** spirit—strong, resilient, and striving for more.

Remember, building a "rich-ass life" isn't a destination; it's a journey. There will be challenges, setbacks, and moments when you want to throw in the towel. But when you're tested, you discover your true strength in those moments. You tap into the "Workout" pillar, building resilience and mental toughness through adversity.

So, get after it. Embrace the discomfort, push past your limits, and never, ever give up on the life you were meant to live. The world needs your gifts, talents, and unique brand of brilliance. Now, go out there and create a life that's so extraordinary that it makes even the haters stop and stare. Become the **WARRIOR** you were born to be.

Alright, we've covered a lot of ground in this chapter. We've explored what it really means to live a "rich-ass life," and I've shared some stories and strategies to help you start designing a life that lights you up. But before we move on, let's take a moment to recap the key takeaways and the nuggets of wisdom you can apply in your life right now.

CHAPTER 12 TAKEAWAYS

- **Redefine Wealth:** True wealth isn't about the size of your bank account; it's about the richness you cultivate in every area of your life. Focus on building a life abundant in love, purpose, growth, and impact. This is the essence of "Integration"—aligning your external success with your internal fulfillment.

- **Embrace Sacrifice:** The path to an extraordinary life is paved with extraordinary sacrifices. Be willing to let go of the things that no longer serve you, whether it's a dead-end job, a toxic relationship, or a limiting belief. Short-term discomfort leads to long-term fulfillment. This is the "Workout" pillar—pushing past your comfort zone to achieve greatness.

- **Face Your Fears:** Fear is a liar, a dream-stealer that keeps you in mediocrity. The antidote to fear is massive, consistent action. Step into the arena, even when terrified, and watch your fears shrink in the face of your courage. This is "Ownership" at its finest—taking control of your life and refusing to be ruled by fear.

- **Build a Strong Foundation:** Surround yourself with people who lift you higher, challenge you to grow, and celebrate your victories. Cultivate a foundation of unshakable faith, whether in a higher power, in yourself, or in the love and support of your pack. This is the power of Relationships—the unwavering support system that allows you to conquer any challenge.

- **Design Your "Rich-Ass Life":** Get crystal clear on what you want and what a truly fulfilling life looks like. Write it in vivid detail, and let that vision be your North Star. Then, take consistent action to make that vision a reality. This is "Reach" in its purest form—setting your sights on a goal and relentlessly pursuing it.

- **Practice Gratitude:** Gratitude is the ultimate abundance magnet. When you focus on the good and appreciate the blessings in your life, you open yourself up to receiving even more. Make gratitude a daily practice, and watch your life transform. This is "Awareness" at work—recognizing and appreciating the good already in your life.

- **Embrace Financial Literacy:** Financial well-being is crucial to a rich-ass life. Educate yourself about money, develop good financial habits, and use it as a tool to create the life you want.

Remember, living a "rich-ass life" is a journey, not a destination. There will be ups and downs, triumphs and challenges. But if you stay committed to growth, surround yourself with the right people, and keep taking action toward your vision, you'll create a life beyond your wildest dreams. So keep pushing, keep growing, and keep shining your light. The world needs more people like you, living rich-ass lives and inspiring others to do the same. Embrace the **WARRIOR** within, and let it guide you to a life of purpose, abundance, and impact.

You've explored the core principles of building a truly rich life: redefining wealth, embracing sacrifice, facing your fears, building a strong foundation, designing your ideal life, practicing gratitude, and embracing financial literacy. Now, tie all these concepts together and discover the transformative power of Total Recreation. Watch our "Total Recreation" video at Elliott Training Academy (ETA). Scan the QR code to watch the video and begin building your rich-ass life today.

CHAPTER 13

WORKOUT

ACTIVATE YOUR WARRIOR BODY

Let's talk about the foundation of everything—the "Workout" pillar. This isn't about getting ripped or looking good in a swimsuit, though that's a nice bonus. This is about building a foundation of strength, resilience, and unwavering energy to fuel every aspect of your life. This is about activating your **WARRIOR** body, forging a temple of power that can withstand any storm and conquer any challenge.

THE 4% COMMITMENT: YOUR NON-NEGOTIABLE INVESTMENT

Listen up because this is non-negotiable. I'm talking about dedicating 4% of your day—just one hour—to physical activity. That's it. One hour. No excuses. This isn't a luxury; it's an investment in your success, well-being, and future. As John Ratey, MD, explains in *Spark: The Revolutionary New Science of Exercise and the Brain*, this one hour isn't just about physical health; it's a powerful tool for sharpening your mind, improving your mood, and boosting your overall cognitive function.

You might be thinking, "Andy, I'm busy. I don't have time for that." Bullshit. We all have 24 hours in a day. You're telling me you can't carve out one hour for the most important person in your life—YOU?

This isn't about hitting the gym and becoming a bodybuilder. It's about moving your body, pumping your blood, and activating those feel-good chemicals in your brain. It's about building a foundation of physical strength that translates into mental toughness and resilience. This is your "Workout," your daily ritual of self-improvement. It's a testament to your Ownership, taking control of your physical and mental well-being.

FUELING THE FERRARI: TREAT YOUR BODY LIKE A HIGH-PERFORMANCE MACHINE

Now, let's talk about fuel. You wouldn't put cheap gas in a Ferrari, would you? So why would you put junk food in your body, the most high-performance machine you'll ever own? Like a high-performance engine requires premium fuel, your body needs high-quality nutrition to function optimally.

Nutrition is crucial. It's about fueling your body with the nutrients it needs to perform at its peak. It's about treating your body like its temple, honoring it with healthy, wholesome foods that will energize, strengthen, and keep you firing on all cylinders. This aligns with the Awareness pillar, which is understanding your body's needs and providing it with the fuel it needs to thrive. As Catherine Shanahan, MD, points out in *Deep Nutrition*, food directly impacts your gene expression, influencing everything from your energy levels to your risk of chronic disease.

Here are a few practical tips for fueling your Ferrari:

- **Prioritize whole, unprocessed foods:** Focus on fruits, vegetables, lean proteins, and healthy fats. These nutrient-rich foods provide the building blocks for a strong, healthy body and mind.

- **Limit processed foods, sugar, and unhealthy fats:** These foods will slow you down, drain your energy, and sabotage your progress.

Research consistently shows a link between processed food consumption and various health problems, from obesity and heart disease to cognitive decline. (See *The China Study* by T. Colin Campbell for more on this).

- **Hydrate like a mofo:** Water is essential for optimal performance. Carry a water bottle with you everywhere and sip on it throughout the day. Dehydration can lead to fatigue, decreased cognitive function, and impaired physical performance.

- **Meal prep like a boss:** Prepare your meals in advance so you're not tempted to grab fast food or unhealthy snacks when you're short on time.

Remember, your body is your temple. Treat it with respect, and it will reward you with energy, strength, and vitality.

THE DO NOT DISTURB ZONE: UNLEASH THE POWER OF FOCUS

When you're working out, it's time to go dark. Put your phone on "Do Not Disturb," silence notifications, and eliminate all distractions. This dedicated focus time allows you to connect with your body, push your limits, and tap into a state of flow, as described by Mihaly Csikszentmihalyi in his book *Flow: The Psychology of Optimal Experience*.

This isn't just about maximizing your physical gains but building mental toughness. When you can shut out the noise and focus on the task, you develop a level of discipline and concentration that will carry over into every area of your life. This aligns with Cal Newport's "deep work" concept in his book *Deep Work: Rules for Focused Success in a Distracted World*. This is the **WARRIOR'S** focus, the unwavering concentration that allows them to conquer any challenge.

And here's the science behind it: intense exercise releases a cocktail of feel-good chemicals in your brain—dopamine, oxytocin, and serotonin. These chemicals boost your mood, reduce stress, and improve your well-being. It's a biological reward for pushing yourself, a natural high that will keep you returning for more. This is the "Workout" pillar—activating your body and mind for peak performance. I learned this in the book, "Leaders Eat Last" by Simon Sinek.

BEYOND THE PHYSICAL:
THE MIND-BODY CONNECTION

Listen up because this is important. Working out isn't just about building physical strength but also mental and emotional stability. This mind-body connection is crucial for overall well-being and peak performance.

When you push your physical limits, you build resilience — the ability to bounce back from setbacks and keep going even when things get tough. You develop a "can-do" attitude that permeates every aspect of your life. This resonates with the findings in *The Resilience Factor* by Karen Reivich and Andrew Shatté, which outlines key strategies for developing resilience. This resilience is a hallmark of the **WARRIOR** spirit, the ability to rise above challenges and emerge stronger.

Working out also reduces stress, improves sleep, and boosts your mood. It's a natural antidepressant and anxiety reliever, helping you manage the inevitable ups and downs of life with greater ease and grace. This aligns with the "Integration" pillar, creating a harmonious balance between physical, mental, and emotional well-being. Numerous studies published in journals like the *Journal of Clinical Psychiatry* have demonstrated the effectiveness of exercise in reducing symptoms of depression and anxiety.

Let's remember confidence. When you look good, you feel good, and when you feel good, you perform well. Working out helps you build a strong, healthy body that you're proud of. That confidence radiates outwards, impacting every area of your life. This is about owning your physical presence, embracing the warrior within, and projecting an aura of strength and confidence that commands respect.

ACTIONABLE STEPS:
BUILDING YOUR WARRIOR WORKOUT ROUTINE

Alright, let's get practical. Here's a step-by-step guide to creating a workout routine that will activate your inner beast:

1. WARM-UP
Prepare your body for action with 5-10 minutes of light cardio, like jogging or jumping jacks, followed by dynamic stretching, such as arm circles

and leg swings. A proper warm-up increases blood flow to your muscles, preparing them for the workout and reducing the risk of injury.

2. WORKOUT

Choose exercises that target all major muscle groups, including squats, lunges, push-ups, pull-ups, and core work. Focus on proper form and gradually increase the intensity and duration of your workouts over time. You can also find great workout routines in our Elliott Training Academy members area. Check out the resources at the end of the book.

3. COOL-DOWN

Finish your Workout with 5-10 minutes of static stretching, holding each stretch for 20-30 seconds. Cooling down helps your body transition back to a resting state, reducing muscle soreness and promoting flexibility.

Remember, consistency is key. Aim for at least 30 minutes of moderate-intensity exercise most days of the week, or follow the 4% rule and dedicate one hour daily. As Michael Hyatt emphasizes in *The Power of Accountability*, tracking your progress and having an accountability partner can significantly increase your chances of sticking to your workout routine. This is your "Workout," your non-negotiable investment in your physical and mental well-being.

ANDY'S WORKOUT RITUAL:
A GLIMPSE INTO THE WARRIOR'S ARSENAL

Let me give you a peek into my workout routine, the rituals that keep me strong, focused, and ready to conquer the day.

- **The 5 AM Club:** Warriors, I'm up before sunrise. This is my time to connect with God, set my intentions for the day, and activate my body and mind.

- **Cold Plunge Power:** Jacqueline and I start our day with a cold plunge. It shocks the system but wakes you up, boosts circulation, and builds mental toughness. Plus, it's a little competition between us—I always have to stay in longer than she does.

- **Intense Training:** My workouts are short, intense, and focused. I'm not in the gym to socialize; I'm there to work. I push myself to the limit, knowing that every rep, every set, is building the **WARRIOR** within.

- **Fueling the Machine:** I prioritize nutrition. I feel my body with whole, unprocessed foods that give me the energy and nutrients I need to perform at my peak.

- **Mental Game Strong:** I visualize my goals, focus on my "why," and remind myself that every Workout is a step closer to becoming the the best version of myself.

Remember, your workout routine should be tailored to your needs and goals. Experiment, find what works for you, and stick to it like glue. This is your "Workout," personal journey to physical and mental mastery.

WORKOUT STORIES:
FROM THE TRENCHES TO THE TOP

Now, let me share a few stories that illustrate the power of the Workout pillar in action. These are real-world examples of how prioritizing physical fitness can transform your life, your business, and your impact on the world.

MY NON-NEGOTIABLES:
THE GRIND DOESN'T STOP

Let's talk about accountability. Do you want to know how I went from a skinny kid with a stutter to dominating sales and building a nine-figure business? It wasn't by wishing and hoping. It was by setting non-negotiables and standards so high I was almost scared to fail. And then? I attached the consequences. Real consequences. Because let's be honest, we all need a little kick in the ass sometimes to keep us moving forward.

I had this simple rule when selling cars: 3 cars, 200 calls, 3 miles. Every single day, I had to sell three cars. I had to make 200 cold calls if I didn't hit that number. And if I whiffed on both? I laced up my running shoes— which I strategically left on the front porch as a constant reminder—and ran three miles. Rain or shine, sick or tired, those three miles were happening. I hated running with a passion, but I hated failing even more. That was my "Workout," not just for my body but for my mind. It was about building discipline, resilience, and an unwavering commitment to my goals. It was about proving to myself that I could push through discomfort and achieve anything I set my mind. This was a direct application of the Ownership pillar, taking full responsibility for my results and holding myself accountable.

And let me tell you, those three miles weren't just about physical punishment. They were a mental reset, a chance to clear my head, reflect on what I could have done differently, and recommit to crushing it the next day. It was about turning that initial pain and frustration into fuel, into a burning desire to prove myself right.

This wasn't something my manager imposed on me. This was self-inflicted accountability. I knew I needed that extra push, that consequence hanging over my head, to keep me from getting complacent. Because, let's be real, comfort is the enemy of progress. And in the sales world, you're dying if you're not growing.

This principle of non-negotiables extends beyond just sales. It applies to every area where you want to grow significantly. Want to get in better shape? Set a non-negotiable workout schedule and attach a consequence to missing it. Want to build a stronger relationship with your spouse? Set a non-negotiable date night and stick to it, no matter what. Want to deepen your faith? Set a non-negotiable time for prayer or meditation and make it a sacred ritual. This is about owning your life and creating the reality you desire.

The key is to make those non-negotiables specific, measurable, and achievable. And the consequences? They have to be something you genuinely don't want to do. That's what makes them effective. It's about creating a system that keeps you moving forward, even when you don't feel like it. It's about embracing the **WARRIOR** spirit and becoming the unstoppable force you were born to be. This ties into the Reach pillar, setting a course for a life of purpose and impact.

I still use this principle in my business today. Every evening, the entire company goes for a run. It's a non-negotiable. It's part of our culture, a ritual reinforcing our commitment to physical and mental toughness. And it's not just about the physical benefits. It's about camaraderie, the shared experience of pushing ourselves beyond our limits. It's about building that brotherhood, that unbreakable bond that makes us unstoppable as a team. This is the power of Relationships.

And when new team members join, they sign a "mental toughness waiver." It's a symbolic agreement that they're willing to be pushed, challenged, and held to a higher standard. It's about embracing the discomfort of growth and committing to becoming the best versions of themselves. It's about stepping onto the **WARRIOR'S** path, where mediocrity is not an option.

So, what are your non-negotiables? What standards are you willing to die for? What consequences will keep you moving forward, even when you don't feel like it? It's time to get real with yourself, set the bar high, and commit to the grind. Because that's how you break bloodlines, shatter limitations, and create a life that most people only dream of. That's the **WARRIOR** way.

THE MENTAL TOUGHNESS WAIVER: NO EXCUSES, ONLY EXECUTION

Let's talk about mental toughness. It's the bedrock of the **WARRIOR** Code, the unwavering resolve that separates those who conquer from those who crumble. It's the grit in your gut, the fire in your soul, the refusal to blink in the face of adversity. And it's not something you're born with; it's something you forge, day in and day out, through relentless discipline and unwavering commitment.

In my world, mental toughness isn't just a nice-to-have; it's a non-negotiable. It's so ingrained in our company culture that we have a "Mental Toughness Waiver." Every single person who joins our team signs it. It's a symbolic agreement, a declaration of war against mediocrity, a commitment to push beyond their limits and embrace the suck.

Think about that for a second. A Mental Toughness Waiver. How many companies out there have something like that? None. Because most companies are afraid to push their people, afraid to challenge them, afraid to demand greatness. But not me. True growth lies outside the comfort zone, in the crucible of challenge and adversity. And I'm not scared to take my team there, to forge them into the **WARRIORS** they were born to be. This aligns perfectly with the Workout pillar, pushing beyond physical limits to build mental resilience.

This waiver isn't about allowing me to be a jerk or abuse my team. It's about creating an environment of accountability, where excuses are unacceptable, and execution is everything. It's about building a culture where everyone is committed to becoming their best version, day in and day out.

This commitment to growth is a testament to the Ownership pillar, taking full responsibility for our individual and collective success.

Mental toughness is the key to overcoming vices, battling adversities, and achieving the impossible. It allows you to keep pushing when every fiber of your being wants to quit. It will enable you to get back up after getting knocked down, stronger and more determined than ever. It's the cornerstone of the **WARRIOR** spirit, the unwavering resolve to conquer any challenge that stands in your way.

My wife, Jacqueline, is a master of mental toughness. She doesn't feed me ice cream; she challenges me. She doesn't feed me ice cream when I feel sorry for myself; she gives me the cold, hard truth. And you know what? I need that. I crave it. Because I know that true growth comes from confronting reality head-on, not hiding from it. This is about surrounding yourself with the right Relationships, with people who will push you to be better, even when it's uncomfortable.

Jacqueline always says, "Do you want me to treat you like a three-, four-, or five-year-old and make you feel better? Or do you want me to treat you like the badass you tell me you are and give you the cold, hard truth?" I always choose the truth, even when it stings. Because I know that pain teaches that discomfort is a compass pointing toward growth, this is about embracing the Recreate pillar, shedding the old, weak self, and forging a new, more powerful identity.

This mentality is essential for building a bloodline-breaker mindset. It's about rejecting victimhood, refusing to make excuses, and taking full responsibility for your life. It's about developing that calloused sensitivity and the ability to withstand life's inevitable blows without crumbling. It's about becoming the rock, the unwavering force your family, team, and clients can rely on. This unwavering strength and support is a key element of the Relationships pillar, building an unbreakable tribe that will stand by you through thick and thin.

So, are you ready to sign your Mental Toughness Waiver? Are you ready to commit to a life of no excuses, only execution? Are you ready to embrace the discomfort of growth and forge into the unstoppable force you were born to be? The choice is yours. But remember, the **WARRIOR'S** path is not for the faint of heart. It's for those willing to fight for what they believe in, push through the pain, and emerge victorious. It's about activating your inner **WARRIOR** and claiming the life you deserve. It's about leaving a legacy of strength, resilience, and unwavering faith. This is the essence of the Reach pillar, striving to make an impact that extends far beyond your own life. So, what do you say? Are you in?

JACQUELINE'S "COMFORTABLE" CONFRONTATION: A WARRIOR'S WAKE-UP CALL

I was 39, making a serious bank, running my company like a boss, and feeling good about myself. On the surface, I had it all: a beautiful family, a successful career, and all the outward signs of success. But beneath the surface, something was off. I was going through the motions, existing instead of truly living. I was losing my edge, my hunger, that **WARRIOR** spirit that had driven me to achieve everything I had.

And then, Jacqueline stepped in and changed the game. She didn't sugarcoat it; she didn't try to spare my feelings. She laid it all out, raw and real like only a **WARRIOR'S** battle mate can. She told me I wasn't present, that I was neglecting my family, and that I was becoming comfortable.

"We've learned to live without you," she said. Those words hit me hard. She explained that I was never truly there, always mentally at work, even physically at home. My mind was constantly racing, chasing the next deal, the next dollar, the next victory. I was missing out on the precious moments with my family, the very reason I was working so hard in the first place.

And then, she delivered the knockout blow. She reached over, grabbed my love handle—yep, I had a little tire around my midsection back then—and said, "You're comfortable."

Comfortable. That word stung. It was a direct hit to my ego, a stark reminder that I was settling for a life that was a fraction of what I could. I had become complacent, losing that fire in my belly, that relentless drive that had propelled me to success.

"You think that's what I wanted when I married you?" she asked. "I could have married any man. I chose you. You promised me the ride of a lifetime, and all you're doing is talking about being better at work."

She wasn't attacking me; she was waking me up. She reminded me of the man I had promised to be, the **WARRIOR** she had fallen in love with. She saw the potential within me, the greatness I was capable of, and she refused to let me settle for less.

That night, I went into the garage, worked out for four hours, shaved my head—I needed a physical change to reflect the mental transformation I was about to undergo—and made a decision that changed my life forever. I was done with comfort, complacency, and the old Andy.

It was time to unleash the **WARRIOR** within, to reclaim my edge, and to become the man I was destined to be. And let me tell you, it was the best damn decision I ever made. Because on the other side of comfort is where the real magic happens, where you tap into a level of power, purpose, and passion you never knew existed. And that, my friend, is the essence of Total Recreation.

These stories are a testament to the power of the Workout pillar. It's not just about physical fitness; it's about building a foundation of strength, resilience, and unwavering energy to fuel every aspect of your life. So, embrace the Workout, activate your inner beast, and watch as your life transforms before your very eyes.

In Chapter 20, I will provide step-by-step instructions for creating your **WARRIOR Framework**. For now, keep grinding!

You've learned about the critical importance of the "Workout" pillar, understanding how physical fitness fuels success, resilience, and unwavering energy. Now, take the next step and learn to invest in yourself, prioritizing your well-being to unlock your full potential. Watch our "Self Investing" video at Elliott Training Academy (ETA). Scan the QR code to watch the video and begin activating your WARRIOR body today.

CHAPTER 14

AWARENESS

KNOW YOUR BATTLEFIELD

This is where the rubber meets the road, where you stop sleepwalking through life and start seeing things with the clarity of a freaking hawk. This is where you become a **WARRIOR**, not just in business, but in every damn aspect of your existence.

THE WARRIOR'S EYE

Awareness. It's the second pillar of the **WARRIOR Framework**; let me tell you, it's the foundation of everything. Think about it like this: a warrior doesn't just charge into battle blindfolded, swinging wildly. They study the terrain, assess the enemy, and know their strengths and weaknesses. They see clearly. Awareness is about developing the warrior's eye, that laser-sharp focus that allows you to clearly see yourself, your surroundings, and your challenges. This "warrior's eye" is akin to what researchers like Tasha Eurich describe as developing internal and external self-awareness—understanding how you see yourself and others perceive you.

Without Awareness, you're just stumbling around in the dark, reacting to whatever life throws your way. But with it, you become a strategic mastermind, making calculated moves, anticipating obstacles, and conquering every damn challenge that stands in your path. It's the difference between being a victim of circumstance and being the architect of your destiny.

THE POWER OF QUESTIONS

Now, how do you develop this Warrior's Eye? It starts with asking yourself the tough questions and engaging in what Donald Schön calls "reflective practice." The questions most people are too afraid to even think about, let alone answer. I'm talking about the questions that make you squirm in your seat, which force you to confront the uncomfortable truths about yourself and your life. This is where the real growth happens, where you peel back the layers of bullshit and get to the core of who you are and what you want.

Here's the thing: most people avoid these questions like the plague. They'd rather live in blissful ignorance than face the hard truths about themselves. But let me tell you something: ignorance isn't bliss. It's a prison. And the only way to break free is to confront your demons head-on. Ask yourself these questions, and be brutally honest with the answers. Write them down. Don't sugarcoat it. Don't make excuses. Just get real with yourself.

- What are my biggest weaknesses? Where am I falling short?

- What am I afraid of? What's holding me back?

- What are my limiting beliefs? What lies am I telling myself?

- Who do I want to be? What kind of legacy do I want to leave behind?

- What should I be doing that I know I should be doing?

- Who am I trying to please? Am I living for myself or others?

- What's one thing I can do today to get closer to my goals?

These are just a few examples, but you get the idea. Dig deep, get uncomfortable, and uncover the truths that will free you.

SEEKING THE TRUTH

Here's another crucial piece of the puzzle: seeking feedback from others. I know, I know. Nobody likes to be criticized. But let me tell you something: constructive criticism is one of the most valuable gifts you can receive. It's like having a personal trainer for your soul, pushing you to grow, identifying your blind spots, and helping you become the best version of yourself. This aligns with Tasha Eurich's research, which emphasizes the importance of external self-awareness—understanding how others see you.

The key is to be open to it. Don't get defensive. Don't make excuses. Just listen—really listen. And then ask clarifying questions. Make sure you understand the feedback and how you can use it to improve. This is about embracing the warrior's humility and willingness to learn and grow, even when uncomfortable.

Think about it like this: you're a warrior preparing for battle. Wouldn't you want your fellow warriors to point out any flaws in your armor or weaknesses in your strategy? Of course you would! Because their feedback could save your life. The same principle applies to life. The feedback you receive from others can help you identify and overcome your blind spots, avoid costly mistakes, and achieve your goals faster.

UNMASKING THE ENEMY

Now, let's talk about the enemy within—your limiting beliefs. These insidious little voices in your head tell you you're not good enough, you'll never make it, or you're not worthy of success. They are the shackles that bind you to mediocrity, the chains that keep you from reaching your full potential. These limiting beliefs often stem from cognitive biases, like confirmation bias, where we tend to favor information that reinforces what we already believe, even if it's not true.

These beliefs are often deeply rooted, stemming from childhood experiences, societal conditioning, or past failures. But here's the good news: you can break free. As Aaron Beck, the pioneer of Cognitive Behavioral Therapy (CBT), suggests, you can identify, challenge, and ultimately change these negative thought patterns. You can unmask these enemies and replace them with empowering truths. It starts with identifying these beliefs. What are the negative thoughts that constantly replay in your head? Write them down. Get them out of your head and onto paper.

Once you've identified your limiting beliefs, it's time to challenge them. Ask yourself, "Is this thought really true? What evidence do I have to support it? What would happen if I chose to believe the opposite?" This is about taking Ownership of your thoughts and refusing to be a victim of your negative self-talk.

Then, replace those limiting beliefs with empowering affirmations. Statements that reflect the truth of who you are and your capabilities. Repeat these affirmations daily, write them down, and say them out loud. The more you reinforce these positive thoughts, the more they'll take root in your subconscious mind and shape your reality.

THE CLARITY ADVANTAGE

When you develop the Warrior's Eye, you gain a massive advantage in the game of life. You see things more clearly, make better decisions, and manage your emotions more effectively. In his groundbreaking work on emotional intelligence, Daniel Goleman highlights self-awareness as a cornerstone of this ability. You become a strategic mastermind, navigating the battlefield of life with confidence and precision.

Increased self-awareness leads to:

- **Greater Clarity:** You know what you want, stand for, and where you're going.

- **Improved Decision-Making:** You make choices aligned with your values and goals.

- **Enhanced Emotional Intelligence:** You manage your emotions effectively, even under pressure. As Goleman suggests, this emotional intelligence includes self-awareness, self-regulation, motivation, empathy, and social skills.

ACTIONABLE STEPS

Here's a guided exercise to help you identify your limiting beliefs and replace them with empowering affirmations:

- **Identify a Limiting Belief:** Choose one negative thought that often holds you back.

- **Challenge the Belief:** Ask yourself, "Is this thought really true? What evidence do I have to support it?"

- **Create an Empowering Affirmation:** Write a positive statement that reflects the opposite of your limiting belief.

- **Repeat and Reinforce:** Say your affirmation out loud every day, write it down, and visualize yourself living in alignment with it.

ANDY'S AWARENESS JOURNEY

Let me share a little bit about my journey with Awareness. It wasn't always pretty. For years, I was blind to my weaknesses, my ego running the show. I thought I had it all figured out, but the truth was, I was sabotaging myself left and right. As Carol Dweck describes it, I operated with a fixed mindset, believing my abilities were static and unchangeable.

It took a serious wake-up call from Jacqueline to shake me out of my complacency. She called me out on my bullshit, forced me to confront my limiting beliefs, and challenged me to become the man I was meant to be. It was painful but also the most important lesson I've ever learned. It forced me to embrace a growth mindset, recognizing that my potential was not predetermined but something I could cultivate and expand through dedication and hard work.

Through that experience, I discovered the power of self-reflection, the importance of seeking feedback, and the transformative power of challenging my limiting beliefs. It was a journey of self-discovery that changed my life forever. The concept of neuroplasticity, the brain's ability to reorganize itself by forming new neural connections throughout life, gave me hope and reinforced the idea that I could rewire my thinking and create lasting change.

I was 39, making serious bank, one of the top car sales managers in the country, and feeling pretty damn good about myself. On the surface, I had it all: a beautiful family, a successful career, and all the outward signs of success. But beneath the surface, something was off. I was going through the motions, existing instead of truly living. I was losing my edge, my hunger, that **WARRIOR** spirit that had driven me to achieve everything I had.

And then, Jacqueline stepped in and changed the game. She didn't sugar-coat it; she didn't try to spare my feelings. She laid it all out, raw and honest, like only a **WARRIOR'S** battle mate can. She told me I wasn't present, that I was neglecting my family, and that I was becoming comfortable.

"We've learned to live without you," she said. Those words hit me hard. She explained that I was never truly there, always mentally at work, even physically at home. My mind was constantly racing, chasing the next deal, the next dollar, the next victory. I was missing out on the precious moments with my family, the very reason I was working so hard in the first place.

I was in every picture—great, right? The sad part is that I didn't remember most of the moments when they were taken…

And then, she delivered the knockout blow. She reached over, grabbed my love handle—yep, I had a little tire around my midsection back then—and said, "You're comfortable."

Comfortable. That word stung. It was a direct hit to my ego, a stark reminder that I was settling for a life that was a fraction of what I could. I had become complacent, losing that fire in my belly, that relentless drive that had propelled me to success.

"You think that's what I wanted when I married you?" she asked. "I could have married any man. I chose you. You promised me the ride of a lifetime, and all you're doing is talking about being better at work."

It was time to unleash the **WARRIOR** within, to reclaim my edge, and to become the man I was destined to be. And let me tell you, it was the best damn decision I ever made. Because on the other side of comfort is where the real magic happens, where you tap into a level of power, purpose, and passion you never knew existed. And that, my friend, is the essence of Total Recreation.

JACQUELINE'S STORY:
FROM EAST SAN JOSE TO EMPIRE BUILDER

Jacqueline's journey starts in East San Jose, a tough neighborhood where gang violence and broken families are the norm. She grew up feeling like an outsider, the kid everyone pitied because her parents were the first in their families to divorce. That "failure in my DNA" mentality took root early, shaping her perspective and holding her back for years. It made her cold, closed off, and afraid to dream big.

When we met, she was self-sufficient, incredibly powerful, and independent, yet something ignited within her. She saw the potential for a different life, a life of purpose, passion, and impact. Together, we decided to break free from those generational curses and rewrite our family's DNA.

Building The Elliott Group wasn't some fairy tale. It was a war, a constant battle against doubt, skepticism, and resistance. Our families didn't understand our vision; they thought we were crazy for selling our house, cars, and everything we owned to invest in our dreams. We slept on mattresses, struggled to make ends meet, and faced countless setbacks. But we never gave up. We had a mission, a burning desire to change lives and build a brotherhood of **WARRIORS**. We knew that God had our backs; that was all our needed fuel.

One of the key lessons we learned early on was the importance of protecting our vision. We stopped sharing our dreams too soon with people who couldn't understand them, people who would only try to tear us down. We focused on building our tribe, surrounding ourselves with like-minded individuals who believed in our mission. We shared our sacrifices with our kids, not to burden them but to plant seeds of greatness in their minds. We taught them we are against the world and can overcome any obstacle together.

Jacqueline's growth is a testament to the power of Awareness. She recognized her limiting beliefs, confronted her past, and consciously decided to rewrite her story. She embraced the **WARRIOR** within, which allowed her to become the powerhouse she is today. She's not just my wife; she's my battle mate, my ride-or-die, the woman who inspires me to push harder, reach higher, and never settle for less than I'm capable of.

Her story is a reminder that no matter where you come from or what you've been through, you can break free from your past, rewrite your DNA, and create a life beyond your wildest dreams. So, take Jacqueline's story to heart, let it fuel your fire, and become the **WARRIOR** you were born to be because the world is waiting for you to rise.

I RAN OUT OF GAS: A WARRIOR'S HUMBLING MOMENT

So, picture this: I'm cruising down the highway, the sun's shining, tunes cranked, and feeling like a million bucks. I'm in the zone, thinking about all the lives we're changing, the empire we're building, and the warriors we're creating. I'm feeling unstoppable like the world is my oyster.

And then, BAM! The car sputters, coughs, and dies. Dead as a doornail. Right there on the side of the highway, like some rookie mistake. I ran out of gas.

Now, Jacqueline usually handles the gas situation. It's not something I typically worry about. My mind is usually focused on bigger things, like conquering the world and leaving a legacy of greatness. But that day, I was on my own, and I got so caught up in the momentum of everything that I completely spaced it. I was so focused on the destination that I forgot to check the damn fuel gauge.

It was a humbling moment, a slap in the face from the universe, reminding me that even **WARRIORS** can get caught slipping. It was a lesson in Awareness, a reminder that even the smallest oversights can derail your progress, no matter how big your vision or how strong your drive is.

And to make matters worse, Jacqueline didn't come to my rescue. She usually bails me out of these situations, but she sent one of the guys that day. It was a double dose of humility, a reminder that I needed to step up my game and take responsibility for my damn actions.

But you know what? I learned a valuable lesson that day. I learned that even in moments of failure, even when you get caught with your pants down, there's an opportunity for growth. It's a chance to re-evaluate your priorities, refocus your energy, and recommit to the fundamentals.

It's like in the gym. You can be crushing it, lifting heavy, feeling like a beast, and then you get injured because you got sloppy with your form. It sets you back and forces you to take a step back and re-evaluate your approach.

But it also makes you stronger, more resilient, and more determined than ever to return even better.

That's what the "running out of gas" experience was for me—a **WARRIOR'S** wake-up call. It was a reminder to stay present, focused, and in control of my damn vehicle, both literally and metaphorically. It was a lesson in humility, a lesson in Awareness, and a lesson in the importance of never taking anything for granted. Because in the game of life, like in the game of business, you can't afford to coast on autopilot. You must stay engaged, stay alert, and stay hungry. Because the moment you get comfortable is the moment you start to lose.

THE POWER OF PROXIMITY:
THE PATRICK BET-DAVID INVESTMENT

Look, I'm not afraid to invest in myself. I'm not afraid to spend money on things that will level me up and help me become the best version of myself. And that's why I dropped half a million dollars on training with Patrick Bet-David. Yeah, you heard that right—half a million. Some people might think that's crazy, but let me tell you something: it was the best damn investment I ever made.

See, Patrick's not just some guru spouting motivational bullshit. He's a **WARRIOR** who's built a massive empire from the ground up. He's a strategic mastermind, a master of sales, leadership, and entrepreneurship. And I knew that being in his proximity, soaking up his wisdom, would accelerate my growth in ways I couldn't imagine.

It's not just about the content of his training, although that's valuable as hell. It's about the mindset, the energy, the sheer force of his presence. It's about seeing firsthand how he operates, thinks, and leads. It's about absorbing and integrating that **WARRIOR** energy into my DNA.

Think about it like this: you want to become a world-class athlete. You don't just train by yourself in your garage. You find the best damn coach you can, you surround yourself with other elite athletes, and you immerse yourself in that environment of excellence. That's what I did with Patrick. I invested in myself, I invested in my growth, and I invested in my future.

And let me tell you, the return on that investment has been exponential. It's not just about the money, although that's a factor. It's about the clarity, the confidence, and the unshakeable belief in myself that I gained from being in Patrick's proximity. It's about the relationships I built, the connections I made, and the doors that opened.

So, invest in yourself if you're serious about becoming a **WARRIOR** hungry for growth and ready to take your life to the next level. Find your Patrick Bet-David, surround yourself with greatness, and watch your world explode. Don't be afraid to spend money on your growth, development, and future because the best investment you can ever make is in yourself. And remember, God doesn't call the qualified; He qualifies the called. So step up and answer the call.

Look, I'm not saying this journey is easy. It's going to be the hardest thing you've ever done. But I promise you, it's worth it. Developing the Warrior's Eye unlocks clarity, power, and purpose that will transform your life forever. You become the master of your destiny, the architect of your own rich-ass life. So get after it. The world is waiting for you to rise. And remember, God's got your back every step of the way.

You've explored the power of Awareness, learning how to develop your Warrior's Eye, ask tough questions, seek truth, unmask the enemy within, and gain the clarity advantage. Now, dive deeper into understanding the impact of your inner dialogue. Watch our video "Self Talk" at Elliott Training Academy (ETA). Scan the QR code to watch the video to learn how to manage your self-talk and cultivate an empowerment mindset and continue your journey toward becoming a true WARRIOR.

CHAPTER 15

RELATIONSHIPS

BUILD YOUR UNRECRUITABLE TRIBE

Let's talk relationships! Not just the romantic kind, though those are damn important, too. I'm talking about the whole network of humans you surround yourself with—your family, friends, mentors, business partners, clients, and even the barista who makes your morning coffee. These connections, my friend, are the most valuable currency you'll ever possess. They're the foundation of a rich-ass life, the rocket fuel that propels you toward your wildest dreams.

STRENGTH IN NUMBERS

You might be thinking, "Andy, I'm a lone wolf. I don't need anyone. I can achieve greatness on my own." While I admire your ambition, let me tell you something: that's a load of bull. Even the most successful people in the world didn't get there solo. They had a team, a support system, a tribe of badasses who had their backs and pushed them to be better. Matthew Lieberman explains in Social that our brains are wired to connect and crave relationships. We're not meant to go it alone. Just like a **WARRIOR** needs their unrecruitable army, you need your people.

Think about it: who's going to celebrate your wins with you? Who will pick you up when you fall flat on your face (because, trust me, you will)? Who will challenge you to grow and become the best version of yourself? It ain't gonna be your Instagram followers. You need real-deal connections with people who believe in you, even when you don't believe in yourself. And let me tell you, God puts those people in your life for a reason. Don't ignore those blessings.

THE TRIBE MENTALITY

Building your tribe is more than just collecting contacts; it's about cultivating genuine, deep-rooted relationships with people who share your values and vision. As Patrick Lencioni points out in The Five Dysfunctions of a Team, common pitfalls can sabotage even the most promising teams. You must be aware of these dysfunctions—like lack of trust, fear of conflict, and avoidance of accountability—and actively work to overcome them. It's about surrounding yourself with those who inspire, challenge, and make you want to level up your game. This is your **WARRIOR** network, the foundation of your success.

A true **WARRIOR** tribe member is loyal, trustworthy, and committed to your growth. They're not afraid to tell you the truth, even when it's hard to hear. They celebrate your wins like their own and pick you up when you're down. They're the people who see your potential, even when you can't see it yourself.

INVESTING IN BONDS

Relationships are like plants; they need constant nurturing to thrive. You gotta invest time, energy, and, yes, even some hard conversations, as Chris Voss talks about in Never Split the Difference, to keep those bonds strong. Schedule regular time for coffee dates, phone calls, or even quick text messages. Be present and engaged when you're with someone. Put your phone away, listen actively, and show genuine interest in their lives.

THE LOYALTY FACTOR

Loyalty is earned, not demanded. It's built through shared experiences, mutual respect, and unwavering support. Create a culture of loyalty within your team and your personal life by being the kind of person others want to be loyal to. Be the kind of leader Simon Sinek describes in Leaders Eat Last, the kind who creates a "circle of safety" where people feel valued and protected. Be trustworthy and dependable, and always have their backs.

THE POWER OF CONNECTION

Strong relationships are like gold. They open doors to opportunities you wouldn't have access to otherwise. They provide accountability that keeps you on track and support that helps weather any storm. And let's be real: loneliness is a killer. It's not just an emotional state; it can have serious consequences for your health and well-being, as John T. Cacioppo and William Patrick detail in their book, Loneliness. When you surround yourself with the right people, you create a powerful network that fuels your success and enriches your life.

ACTIONABLE STEPS

Here's the rubber meets the road: Applying Cialdini's six principles of persuasion from Influence can be a game-changer here:

- **Communicate with Clarity:** Be direct, honest, and transparent. Don't beat around the bush or play games.

- **Listen Actively:** Pay attention to what others say verbally and non-verbally. Ask clarifying questions and show genuine interest.

- **Show Appreciation:** Express your gratitude regularly. A simple "thank you" can go a long way. Reciprocity in action.

- **Offer Support:** Be there for your tribe when they need you, both in good times and bad.

- **Invest in Growth:** Encourage and support the growth of those around you. Help them become the best versions of themselves.

ANDY'S TRIBE:
STORIES FROM THE TRENCHES

Let me tell you a few stories about the relationships that have shaped my life and my business:

THE "I'M NOT YOUR BABYSITTER" PHILOSOPHY:
FORGING WARRIORS

Let's be clear: you're not working for the job you want; you're working for the job you're after. That next level, that leadership position, is what you should focus on. And let me tell you something you might not want to hear: sometimes, promotion is a demotion. You can be a badass salesperson, the top performer, or the closer extraordinaire. But you're not a leader if you can't teach what you know or build others up. You're stuck. You gotta be able to train your team, to empower them to be even better than you.

A true sales boss or leader isn't always the best salesperson. They can hang with the best, but their real strength lies in their ability to ignite the fire in others. They can turn a team of 30 people into an unstoppable force.

They create the rhythm, the heartbeat of the company. They walk in, and they just know when something's off. The energy's low. The music's not pumping. The vibe is just… wrong. They smell that shit a mile away, and they fix it. They're not just managing; they're creating heroes.

Do you want your team to be loyal, to give you everything they've got? You gotta change their lives. You gotta be a coach, a mentor, a leader who invests in their growth, not just their production. Idiot business people focus on numbers and the bottom line. They never get close enough to anyone to build real relationships and forge true loyalty. A sales boss knows everyone. They know their team's families, their struggles, their dreams. They help them set goals, not just for their careers, but for their lives.

I tell my team, "Bring your wife, girlfriend, and significant other to our one-on-ones." Some might say, "We don't need them there." Hell, yes, we do. They're part of the team. They have Influence. They're in this fight with us. It's work-life integration, not work-life balance. Zero balance. You gotta include the people who matter most. They're the foundation, the bedrock of everything we do.

We have a chat line in our company. It's a constant stream of communication, support, shared victories, and struggles. Someone will post a video and say, "This changed my life." I'll click on it, even if it's an hour long. I have to watch it. That person is my responsibility. They shared something that moved them and shifted their perspective. I need to know what that is. I need to understand them.

I don't care how much money you make. Are you getting better every day? That's the only metric that truly matters. If you're not growing, you're not with us. If you constantly strive to improve, you'll get where you need to be. Don't make decisions based on money. Build relationships that will last. Treat every customer like they're part of your tribe, like you'll be with them for the next ten years. Do you want your team to be with you in 10 years? Imagine that. The same amazing team a decade from now. What would your business look like? What would your life look like?

I travel all the time. I don't need to babysit my team. I've told them from day one, "I'm not your babysitter." I trust them, but that trust is earned, not given. I'll micromanage until they prove they can handle the responsibility. Then they're on their own, free to fly. Don't give people blind trust. Make them earn it. When you tell people you won't babysit them, it forces them to step up and take ownership. If I must wake you up in the morning, you're not a **WARRIOR**. You're not part of this tribe.

I'm not a boss; I'm a coach. And I'll coach you to be better, push past your limits, and become your best version. The day you get sick of me coaching you, the day you stop wanting to grow, that's the day you're out. You should be lucky someone's coaching, pushing, and believing in you. Most people don't have that. They're surrounded by people who enable their mediocrity, who tell them it's okay to settle. Don't let that be you. Be a **WARRIOR**. Build your tribe. And never, ever settle.

BUILDING UNBREAKABLE BONDS WITH CLIENTS: IT'S MORE THAN JUST A TRANSACTION

This isn't about closing techniques or manipulative tactics. It's about building real relationships, the kind where your clients become part of your tribe, where they trust you, respect you and want to do business with you, not just because of your product but because of who you are.

Remember what I said earlier: whoever cares about the client the most wins. That's the game. It's not about outsmarting them or outmaneuvering them. It's about showing them, proving to them, that you genuinely care about their success, their well-being, and their lives.

My goal isn't just to sell something; it's to make my clients feel more powerful, important, loved, and successful. I want them to feel like they matter and are the most significant people in the room. I want to shower them with love, certainty, and unwavering support.

This isn't about dominance in the traditional sense. It's not about overpowering them or making them feel small. It's about exuding quiet confidence, a certainty from knowing who you are and what you stand for. It's about being a leader, a trusted advisor, someone they can rely on.

When I talk to a client, I'm all in. I'm so sold on the value I bring and the relationship we're building that there's nothing else. They feel that. They feel they'd betray themselves if they went with someone else, even for less money. They chose me not just because of my product but because of the connection we've made.

That's moral authority. That's the power of building genuine relationships. It's not about what you say but who you are. It's about embodying human excellence, about becoming the person others want to be around, do business with, and be like.

People buy in two ways: logically and emotionally. Logically, they might like your product, its features, and its benefits. But emotionally, they have to like you. We dominate our industry because we're liked more than anyone else. We build unbreakable relationships that go beyond the transaction.

How do we do it? We become the example. We live the **WARRIOR** way. We take care of ourselves, our families, our teams. We embody the values we preach. We become the people others want to emulate. We become the people our clients want to be in business with, not just for a day but a lifetime. That's the power of building a tribe. That's the power of genuine connection. That's the power of the **WARRIOR** way.

Relationships are the lifeblood of any successful business and a fulfilling life. As Carol Dweck explains in Mindset, a growth mindset is crucial for building and maintaining these vital connections. Build your tribe wisely, invest in those bonds, and watch your life transform in ways you never thought possible. This is the warrior way. Now, go out there and build your unrecruitable tribe!

You've explored the power of Relationships, understanding how crucial your tribe is to your overall success and well-being. Now, learn to strategically choose the people you surround yourself with to maximize your growth and create a powerful support system. Watch our "Choose Your Circle Carefully" video at Elliott Training Academy (ETA). Scan the QR code to watch the video and start building your unrecruitable tribe today.

RECREATE

FORGE YOUR NEW ARMOR

Look, let's be real. Life isn't a straight shot to the top. It's a damn roller-coaster—twists, turns, ups, downs, the whole shebang. And if you're not constantly evolving, adapting, shedding the old, and embracing the new, you will get left in the dust. This chapter, this whole "Recreate" pillar, is about forging your new armor, becoming the ultimate version of yourself, the **WARRIOR** you were destined to be. It's about taking ownership of your life, rewriting your story, and building a legacy that'll make the haters choke on their damn envy.

THE ART OF REINVENTION

Recreate is all about constantly shedding the old you, the limitations, the beliefs, the habits that no longer serve you. It's about embracing change, evolving, and becoming even more badass than you were yesterday. This process of reinvention is crucial for growth and adaptation, allowing us to reach our full potential.

This isn't some fluffy, feel-good self-help crap. This is about survival. The world's changing faster than ever before. You will get left behind if you're not adapting, learning, and reinventing yourself. This is about reaching your full potential, tapping into that God-given greatness inside you, and becoming the person you were always meant to be.

KILLING THE OLD YOU:
A STEP-BY-STEP GUIDE TO TOTAL ANNIHILATION

Now, let's talk strategy. How do you actually "kill" the old you? It's not about some mystical ritual or overnight transformation. It's a process, a daily grind, a commitment to becoming a better version of yourself, one damn day at a time. It's about embracing the **WARRIOR** within, who takes ownership of their life and refuses to settle for mediocrity. This aligns with Cognitive Behavioral Therapy (CBT) principles, which focus on changing negative thought patterns and behaviors.

Here's the blueprint:

- **Identify the Saboteurs:** Get real with yourself. What habits, beliefs, and behaviors are holding you back? Are you constantly procrastinating? Does negativity surround you? Are you afraid to take risks? Write that shit down. Shine a light on those shadows. This is about "Awareness," brother—knowing your enemy before you can conquer it. This self-reflection is a crucial first step in understanding your self-schemas and how they influence your actions.

- **Challenge the Lies:** Those limiting beliefs you've been carrying around? They're lies. Challenge them. Ask yourself, "Is this really true? Or is this just some bullshit story I've been telling myself?" This process of challenging negative thoughts is a core component of CBT and can lead to significant improvements in mental well-being.[2] Replace those lies with empowering truths. You are capable of greatness. You are worthy of success. You are a freaking **WARRIOR**. Embrace a growth mindset, believing that your abilities and intelligence can be developed through dedication and hard work.

- **Create Your "Burn the Boats" List:** This is about getting radical. What are you willing to sacrifice to create the life you want? What are you ready to let go of—the toxic relationships, the dead-end job, the self-sabotaging habits? Write it down. And then, literally or metaphorically, burn that damn list. There's no going back. This is about commitment, about taking ownership of your destiny.

- **Replace the Bad with the Good:** You've identified the saboteurs and burned the boats. Now, it's time to replace the bad with the good. Develop new habits—remember, small changes, consistently applied, can lead to remarkable results. Cultivate empowering beliefs, and surround yourself with people who lift you higher. This is about "Relationships" and "Integration"—building a support system to empower you on your journey.

- **Take Massive Action:** Knowledge without action is worthless. You've got the plan; now, it's time to execute. Start small, but start now. Take one step every single day toward the life you want. This is about the "Workout" pillar—consistent effort, relentless pursuit, and unwavering commitment. This aligns with actively shaping your environment to support your goals.

UNLEASHING THE WARRIOR WITHIN: EMBRACING THE SUCK

Let's talk about discomfort. Most people run from it like it's the plague. But here's the thing: discomfort is where the magic happens. It's where you grow, learn, and forge the unbreakable spirit of a **WARRIOR**. Stepping outside your comfort zone can lead to increased arousal and, according to the Yerkes-Dodson Law, optimal performance.

Remember when Jacqueline called me out on getting "comfortable"? Man, that stung. But it was the wake-up call I needed. It lit a fire under my ass and forced me to confront the mediocrity I had settled for. It forced me to recreate myself and unleash the **WARRIOR** within. This process of confronting my comfort and complacency was essential for my growth. It pushed me beyond my usual level of arousal and allowed me to tap into a new level of performance.[7]

Here's the deal: if you want to achieve greatness, you have to be willing to embrace the suck. You have to be willing to push past your limits, face your fears, and do the hard things that most people won't. That's how you build mental toughness, resilience, and the unwavering determination to carry you through any challenge. Building resilience is a key component of stress inoculation training, allowing you to develop coping skills and bounce back from adversity.

THE POWER OF EVOLUTION:
NEVER STOP GROWING

The journey of Total Recreation isn't a one-time thing. It's a lifelong commitment to growth, evolution, and self-improvement. It's about constantly seeking knowledge, upgrading your skills, and improving yourself daily.

Think about it like this: you're not just building a business; you're building a legacy. And legacies aren't built overnight. They're built brick by brick, day after day, through consistent effort and unwavering commitment.

LIVING IN ALIGNMENT:
WALKING THE TALK

This is about integrity. It's about aligning your actions with your values and living a life that's authentic to who you are. It's about walking the talk and being the example you want others to follow.

Remember what I said about moral authority? It's not about preaching or pretending to be perfect. It's about living your values so powerfully that it inspires others to raise their damn standards. It's about being the kind of person who walks into a room and commands respect, not because of their title or their bank account, but because of the energy they radiate, the integrity they embody, and the impact they make.

ACTIONABLE STEPS:
YOUR PERSONAL RECREATION ROADMAP

Now, let's get practical. Here's a guided exercise to help you identify and eliminate those limiting beliefs and behaviors holding you back:

> • **The Mirror Exercise:** Look yourself dead in the eye and ask, "Who am I? Who do I want to be? What's stopping me?" Be brutally

honest. This is about "Awareness"—knowing your starting point before you can chart your course.

- **The "I Am" Statements:** Write down five "I am" statements that reflect the person you want to become. "I am confident." "I am successful." "I am a leader." Say these statements out loud every single day. This is about reprogramming your subconscious mind, creating a new identity from the inside out.

- **The Accountability Partner:** Find someone to hold you accountable for your goals. This could be a friend, a mentor, or even a coach. Share your vision with them, and ask them to call you out when you're slipping. This is about "Relationships"—building a support system that will empower you on your journey.

ANDY'S RECREATIONS: MY STORY OF TRANSFORMATION

I've shared bits and pieces of my story throughout this book, but let me give you the unfiltered, no-BS version.

I wasn't always the confident, successful **WARRIOR** you see today. I came from a broken home, struggled with self-doubt, and made a lot of damn mistakes along the way. But through it all, I never gave up on my dream of creating a better life for myself and my family.

One night, Jacqueline and I sat at our kitchen table, surrounded by bills we couldn't pay. We were stressed, exhausted, and ready to throw in the towel. But then, something shifted. We looked at each other and said, "We're not going down like this."

That night, we made a pact. We were going to change our lives, no matter what it took. We were going to break the bloodline of mediocrity and create a legacy of success and abundance for our kids. And we were going to do it together.

We started small. We changed our habits, mindsets, and the people we surrounded ourselves. We embraced discomfort, pushed past our limits, and never stopped learning. We took ownership of our lives and refused to make excuses.

Slowly but surely, things started to change. Our income increased, our relationships thrived, and our confidence soared. We were recreating ourselves from the inside out, becoming the **WARRIORS** we were always meant to be.

RECREATE STORIES: LESSONS FROM THE TRENCHES

Now, let's dive into some specific stories that illustrate the power of Recreate in action. These are real-world examples from my life and the lives of those around me: stories of transformation, resilience, and unwavering commitment to growth.

THE EAGLE REBIRTH

I've always been fascinated by eagles. These majestic creatures, rulers of the sky, embody the warrior's spirit. They're strong, resilient, and fearless. But most people don't know that eagles undergo rebirth, a radical transformation that allows them to soar to even greater heights.

It's called molting. They shed their old, worn, and weathered feathers, making way for new, stronger plumage. It's a painful process, stripping the old to make way for the new. But it's essential for their survival and ability to dominate the skies.

And that, my friends, is what Recreate is all about. It's about shedding the old you—the limitations, the fears, the doubts—and embracing the new, more powerful version of yourself. It's about molting, like the eagle, and emerging stronger, more resilient, and ready to conquer anything life throws your way.

I remember feeling like that eagle, weighed down by old feathers, struggling to stay aloft. I was going through a tough time in my business. We had hit a plateau, and I felt like I was losing my edge. Doubt started creeping in, whispering lies in my ear: "You're not good enough. You're not cut out for this. You're going to fail."

Those negative thoughts were like heavy chains, dragging me down and keeping me from soaring to my full potential. I was losing my **WARRIOR** spirit, forgetting the principles of Ownership and Reach that had brought me this far.

I needed to molt. I needed to shed those old feathers of doubt and fear and embrace the new, stronger version of myself.

So, I did what any self-respecting **WARRIOR** would do. I took action. I dove headfirst into self-development, seeking mentors who had walked the path before me. I devoured books, listened to podcasts, and surrounded myself with people who believed in my vision. I was rebuilding my Relationships, strengthening my tribe, and reminding myself that I wasn't alone in this fight.

I also reconnected with my faith. I prayed for guidance, strength, and courage to face my fears. And you know what? God met me where I was. He reminded me of my purpose, of the impact I was meant to make in the world. He showed me that my struggles weren't a sign of weakness but an opportunity for growth, a chance to molt and emerge stronger than ever.

And then, there was Jacqueline—my rock, my ride-or-die, the woman who always sees the best in me, even when I can't see it myself. She reminded me of the sacrifices we had made together when we had slept on mattresses and driven beat-up cars to chase our dreams. She challenged me to remember my "why" and reconnect with the fire that had driven me from the beginning. She was my constant source of support, my unwavering reminder of the **WARRIOR** within.

With their support and guidance, I started to shed those old feathers. I identified the limiting beliefs holding me back and challenged them. I replaced negative self-talk with affirmations and empowered truths. I embraced discomfort, stepped outside my comfort zone, and took risks I would have never considered. I was molting, painfully but purposefully, just like the eagle.

As I shed the old, the new began to emerge. I rediscovered my passion, drive, and unwavering belief in myself and my vision. I started seeing opportunities where I had once seen obstacles. I reconnected with my team and my tribe, and we soared to new heights together.

The process wasn't easy. Sometimes, I wanted to give up, to crawl back into the comfort of my old feathers. But I kept pushing, molting, and reminding myself of the eagle's example.

Looking back, I can see how essential that period of transformation was. It was my eagle rebirth, a time of shedding the old and embracing the new. It allowed me to become the leader, entrepreneur, and warrior I am today.

So, if you're feeling weighed down and struggling to stay aloft, remember the eagle. Remember the power of Recreate. It's time to molt. It's time to shed the old you and embrace the new. It's time to unleash the **WARRIOR** within and soar to heights you never thought possible.

THE ALMOST-RETURNED COACHING PROGRAM AND JACQUELINE'S "WINNERS GET AN ROI" LESSON

Let me tell you a story about a time I almost made a huge mistake that could have cost me not just money but also my integrity. It was a time when my faith in myself wavered, and I almost let doubt and fear dictate my actions. Thank God for Jacqueline, my rock, my truth-teller, the woman who always knows exactly what I need to hear. This story is about the power of commitment, the importance of getting an ROI on every investment, and the unwavering belief in your potential—even when you're struggling to see it yourself.

It was about five years ago. I had invested in a pretty expensive training program, hoping it would take my business to the next level. But things weren't going as planned. I was hitting roadblocks, frustrated, and doubting myself because I was not very technical. I was in a low place, a moment of weakness, and that's when the old, comfortable Andy started to creep back in.

I told Jacqueline I was thinking about asking for a refund. Even though I had gone through the program a hundred times, it was valuable and life-changing.

She looked at me like I had committed the ultimate sin like I had betrayed myself and everything we stood for. She reminded me of the principle of karma, the energy we put into the world, and how it always comes back to us. She said if I got a refund after receiving value from the program, every customer I ever had would chargeback.

Her words hit me hard. I knew she was right. It wasn't about the money but my integrity, commitment, and **WARRIOR** spirit. I had made a promise to myself, the program, and the people I was meant to serve. And winners, as Jacqueline reminded me, always keep their promises.

She didn't stop there. In her infinite wisdom, Jacqueline taught me a valuable lesson that day. She said, "Winners are winners. Winners get an ROI regardless of the training program." She repeated it three times just to make sure it sunk in.

Her point was simple yet profound. My success wasn't dependent on the program but on me. I was responsible for my ROI, extracting every ounce of value I could from the investment, regardless of the program's quality. Even if the program were terrible, she argued, a true winner, a true **WARRIOR**, would find a way to make it work.

That's Jacqueline's unwavering belief in me, the kind of belief I needed to hear in that moment of weakness. She reminded me of my potential, of the power I had within me to achieve anything I set my mind to. She called me back to the "Ownership" pillar, reminding me I was 100% responsible for my success.

And you know what? She was right. I didn't ask for a refund. I doubled down on my efforts, committed to extracting every bit of value I could from the program, and ultimately achieved the results I was looking for.

That experience taught me a valuable lesson about the importance of commitment, the power of unwavering belief, and the necessity of getting an ROI on every investment, not just financially but in every area of life. It reinforced the **WARRIOR** principles of "Ownership" and "Reach"—taking responsibility for my success and striving to maximize my impact on the world.

It's a lesson I've carried with me ever since. Whenever I face a challenge or feel like giving up, I remember Jacqueline's words: "Winners get an ROI." And I recommit to the grind, to the relentless pursuit of my goals, knowing that I have the power within me to achieve anything I set my mind to.

This story isn't just about a coaching program; it's about a fundamental shift in mindset. Jacqueline's lesson transcended the situation and became a guiding principle in my life and business. It's about taking Ownership of your success, regardless of external circumstances. It's about embracing the **WARRIOR** spirit and refusing to let challenges or setbacks define you. It's about cultivating an unwavering belief in your ability to achieve an ROI on every investment in every area of life.

These stories and moments of transformation prove Recreate is not just a concept; it's a way of life. It's a commitment to constant growth, evolution, and self-improvement. It's about shedding the old you, the limitations, fears, and doubts that have held you back. And it's about stepping into the most powerful, authentic version of yourself, the warrior you were always meant to be.

So, what are you waiting for? It's time to forge your new armor. It's time to Recreate your damn life.

This journey isn't about becoming someone else. It's about becoming more fully yourself, the person God created you to be. It's about stripping away the masks, the facades, and the bullshit and stepping into your authentic truth. It's about unleashing the **WARRIOR** within.

So, take a deep breath, pray for guidance, and take that first step. Kill the old you and give birth to the new. Embrace the process of Total Recreation, and watch as your life transforms before your very eyes. Because on the other side of death is rebirth, and on the other side of fear is freedom. You were made for this. You were made for more. Now go out there and recreate your damn life. I'll be cheering you on every step of the way. Because together, we rise.

You've explored the Recreate pillar, learning to reinvent yourself, kill the old you, embrace discomfort, and unleash your inner WARRIOR. Now, delve deeper into embracing failure as a stepping stone to growth. Watch our "Failure Is The Road" video at Elliott Training Academy (ETA). Scan the QR code to watch the video and begin forging your new armor today.

CHAPTER 17

INTEGRATION

UNIFY YOUR BATTLE PLAN

Alright, let's talk about something crucial to this whole damn Total Recreation journey: Integration. This is not about balance, that fluffy, feel-good buzzword that sets you up for failure. This is about unifying every facet of your life—your mind, body, spirit, family, business, the whole damn enchilada—into a powerful, synergistic force. It's about becoming the holistic **WARRIOR**, the integrated badass who's not just winning in one area but dominating all of them. This is where the rubber meets the road, where you take Ownership of your entire existence and Reach for a level of fulfillment most people only dream of.

WORK-LIFE INTEGRATION, NOT BALANCE

Forget balance. Balance is a myth, a teeter-totter that's always shifting, leaving you feeling like you're constantly falling short. Conversely, Integration is about weaving together the different strands of your life into a seamless tapestry. It's about creating a life where your work fuels your personal life and vice versa, where your passions and priorities are aligned, and where you're showing up as the best version of yourself in every damn arena. Research shows that true work-life integration, instead of mere balance, leads to greater job satisfaction, improved mental health, and enhanced productivity (Kossek & Lautsch, Year).

Here's the deal: Most folks try to compartmentalize their lives—work over here, family over there, and personal time squeezed in between. But that's like trying to build a house with separate foundations. It's unstable, unsustainable, and ultimately sets you up for collapse. Integration is about building one solid foundation that supports every aspect of your life.

THE POWER OF PRESENCE

One of the most powerful tools in your Integration arsenal is presence. Being present means showing up fully in each moment, whether closing a million-dollar deal, coaching your kid's soccer team, or having a heart-to-heart with your spouse. It means putting your phone down, silencing the noise in your head, and giving your undivided attention to the task at hand, the person in front of you, and your experience. This aligns with the principles of mindfulness, a practice shown to enhance focus, emotional regulation, and decision-making by fostering a heightened state of Awareness (Kabat-Zinn, Year). Neuroscience research even supports that regular mindfulness can physically alter the brain, leading to these positive changes (Davidson, Year).

When you're present, you're not just going through the motions; you're truly living. You savor the good moments, learn from the tough ones, and connect with the world on a deeper level. And that, my friend, is the key to a rich-ass life. It's about more than just checking boxes; it's about experiencing the fullness of each moment and extracting every ounce of joy, growth, and connection.

VALUES-DRIVEN BUSINESS

Look, we all want to be successful. But what does success mean? Is it about the size of your bank account, the fancy car in your driveway, or the accolades on your wall? Or is it about something deeper, something more meaningful?

True success is about living a life aligned with my values. It's about building a business that makes me money and makes a difference. It's about using my gifts and talents to serve others, to leave a legacy that matters, and to inspire others to rise alongside me. This is the essence of the "Reach" pillar - extending your impact beyond yourself. Leaders prioritizing purpose and values often correlate positively with employee engagement and organizational performance (Sinek, Year). Creating a values-driven culture can foster a sense of belonging and shared purpose, leading to increased productivity, innovation, and profitability (Collins, Year).

When your business is aligned with your values, work becomes more than just a job; it becomes a calling. You wake up every morning with a fire in your belly, excited to tackle the day and make a real impact. And that, my friend, is the key to long-term fulfillment and sustainable success.

THE SYNERGY ADVANTAGE

When you integrate all aspects of your life, something magical happens. You create synergy, a force multiplier that amplifies your results in every area. Your physical health fuels your mental clarity, your strong relationships provide unwavering support, your sense of purpose drives your business forward, and your business success creates opportunities to make an even bigger impact on the world. It's a virtuous cycle, a self-reinforcing loop that propels you towards your wildest dreams. This concept is supported by research on holistic wellness, emphasizing the interconnectedness of physical, mental, and spiritual well-being (Author, Year). Studies show that improvements in one area, such as physical health, can have a positive ripple effect on other areas, like mental clarity and emotional resilience, leading to a synergistic improvement in overall well-being.

And here's the kicker: Integration leads to greater success and happiness, reduced stress, and a more meaningful existence. When you're living in alignment with your values, when your work and personal life are integrated, you experience a sense of peace, joy, and fulfillment that money can't buy.

ACTIONABLE STEPS

Now, let's get practical. How do you integrate your life? It starts with intentionality. You have to be deliberate about how you spend your time, energy, and focus. Developing resilience and grit—the ability to bounce back from setbacks and persevere through challenges—is also essential for navigating the inevitable obstacles on the path to Integration (Duckworth, Year). Cultivating these traits can empower you to maintain focus and commitment even when faced with adversity (Seligman, Year).

Here's a guided exercise to get you started:

- **Values Audit:** Take some time to reflect on your core values. What truly matters to you? What principles guide your decisions and actions? Write them down.

- **Weekly Schedule Review:** Look at your current weekly schedule. Does it reflect your values? Are you allocating enough time for the things that matter most—family, health, personal growth, and meaningful work?

- **Integration Exercise:** Create a new weekly schedule that integrates all aspects of your life. Block out time for work, family, personal time (hobbies, passions, etc.), self-care (exercise, meditation, etc.), and spiritual practice (prayer, reflection, etc.). Be realistic but also bold. Don't be afraid to experiment and adjust as needed.

ANDY'S INTEGRATED LIFE

For me, Integration is non-negotiable. It's the foundation of my success and the key to my happiness. I've built my business around my family, not vice versa. My kids are a part of my daily life, even when working. They see me hustling, grinding, and pursuing my dreams, and I'm teaching them the value of hard work, dedication, and making a difference in the world.

I'm also fiercely protective of my time with Jacqueline. We have dedicated date nights, work out together, and have daily rituals that keep us connected and aligned. We're a team, a unified front against the world, and our relationship is the bedrock of everything we do.

And let's not forget about my faith. God is at the center of my life, and I start and end each day with prayer and reflection. My faith is the anchor that keeps me grounded, the fuel that keeps me fired up, and the compass that guides my every decision.

THE $100,000 CAR SACRIFICE

Let me tell you about a sacrifice, a real sacrifice, not some symbolic gesture but a down-and-dirty, gut-wrenching decision that changed the trajectory of our lives. This wasn't about giving up something small; this was about letting go of a tangible symbol of success, a symbol we thought we deserved. This was about putting our money where our mouths were, about betting on our vision with everything we had.

This story is about the power of shared sacrifice, a cornerstone of Integration, and a testament to the unwavering commitment it takes to build something truly extraordinary.

We were on the verge of building our dream house. We had the plans, the land, and the financing. We could practically taste the champagne, feel the plush carpet under our feet, and picture ourselves living the high life. We had worked our asses off, and we felt like we had earned it. This was the American dream, culminating years of hustle and sacrifice. This house was more than just bricks and mortar; it symbolized our arrival, a tangible representation of our success.

But then, something shifted. We had a come-to-Jesus moment, a moment of clarity that cut through the fog of our ambition. We realized that this dream house, this symbol of our achievement, was holding us back. It was a distraction, a financial burden that would tie us down and prevent us from fully investing in our true vision. This was a moment of profound

Awareness, a realization that our Relationships and shared vision were more important than any material possession.

So, we made a decision that shocked our friends and family. We sold those $100,000 cars—symbols of our hard-earned success—and poured every penny into our business. We downsized our lifestyle, moved into a small rental, and created our "war room," a space dedicated to our mission where we could pour our hearts and souls into building our dreams.

This wasn't about deprivation; this was about strategic investment. This was about prioritizing our vision, our mission, and our future. It was about taking Ownership of our choices and making the tough decisions that would propel us toward our ultimate goal. It was about recognizing that sometimes, you must sacrifice the good to make room for the great.

And let me tell you, it wasn't easy. There were moments when we questioned our sanity and longed for the comfort and security of that dream house. But we never wavered. We kept our eyes on the prize, fueled by our unwavering belief in our vision and commitment to each other.

This sacrifice, this shared sacrifice, forged an unbreakable bond between us. It strengthened our resolve, deepened our trust, and solidified our commitment to our mission. It was a crucible that tested our limits and forged us into the **WARRIORS** we are today.

And here's the kicker: that sacrifice paid off in spades—not just financially but in every aspect of our lives. It allowed us to focus our energy, time, and resources on building something meaningful. It allowed us to create a business that makes us money and makes a difference in the world. It allowed us to build a life of purpose, passion, and unwavering faith.

This story is not just about cars and houses; it's about the power of shared sacrifice, the importance of aligning your priorities with your values, and the transformative potential of Integration. It's a reminder that sometimes, the greatest rewards come from letting go of what you think you deserve and embracing the discomfort of pursuing something bigger than yourself. It's about having the courage to make the tough choices, the discipline to stay the course, and the unwavering faith that the sacrifices you make today will create a richer, more fulfilling tomorrow.

JACQUELINE STUDYING AT 3:30 AM

Picture this: 3:30 AM. The house is silent, shrouded in the stillness of pre-dawn darkness. Our kids are nestled in their beds, dreaming their innocent dreams. And there, in the dim glow of a bedside lamp, is Jacqueline, my **WARRIOR** queen, not asleep, not resting, but grinding, pushing herself to become the best version of herself. This wasn't some fleeting burst of motivation; this was a nightly ritual, a testament to her unwavering dedication to our family and business. This story isn't just about late-night study sessions; it's a glimpse into the heart and soul of Integration, a demonstration of the unwavering commitment it takes to build a life of true significance.

She's sprawled on the couch, a tangle of limbs and determination, clad in her underwear, surrounded by a fortress of training materials. Her face is buried in a notebook, a pen clutched in her hand, leaving ink stains on the cushions as she scribbles notes. Exhaustion is etched onto her features, but her eyes burn fiercely, a fire that refuses to be extinguished. This isn't just about acquiring knowledge; this is about transformation, about absorbing the wisdom that will fuel her growth and propel her forward on our shared journey. This relentless pursuit of knowledge and this unwavering dedication to self-improvement is a hallmark of the **WARRIOR'S** mindset.

I often stood there, watching her in awe and sometimes in bewilderment, thinking, "What are we doing?" The sacrifices, the long hours, and the constant push to become more often felt surreal, like a dream we were chasing with reckless abandon. But in those quiet moments, in the stillness of the night, I knew exactly what we were doing. We were breaking free from the chains of our past, rewriting our story, and building a future beyond our wildest dreams. We laid the foundation for a legacy of strength, resilience, and unwavering faith. This unwavering focus on a shared vision, this relentless pursuit of a common goal, is the essence of Integration.

Jacqueline wasn't just studying business strategies or sales tactics; she was devouring personal development books, listening to motivational speakers, and immersing herself in the wisdom of mentors who had walked the path before us. She was on a quest for self-discovery to uncover her true potential and become the **WARRIOR** she was always meant to be. This commitment to Total Recreation, to constantly evolving and becoming more, is a key element of the **WARRIOR'S** path.

Those late-night study sessions weren't just about improving our business and strengthening our family. Jacqueline knew that by becoming the best version of herself, she was also becoming a better wife, mother, and leader. She was setting an example for our children, showing them the power of hard work, the importance of pursuing your dreams, and the transformative potential of unwavering dedication. This is the true power of Integration—aligning your personal growth with your family's well-being and creating a ripple effect of positive change.

This image of Jacqueline studying at 3:30 AM is more than just a snapshot in time; it's a symbol of our journey, a testament to the sacrifices we made, the challenges we overcame, and the unwavering commitment we shared. It's a reminder that building a life of significance requires more than just hard work; it requires a relentless pursuit of growth, an unwavering dedication to your vision, and the courage to embrace the discomfort of constant evolution. This is the **WARRIOR'S** way—a path of constant growth, unwavering dedication, and the relentless pursuit of becoming the best version of yourself, not just for yourself but for the people you love and the legacy you want to leave behind.

These stories are not just anecdotes but examples of what's possible when you integrate all aspects of your life. They Show That you can achieve extraordinary success without sacrificing your family, health, or soul. They're a testament to the power of the **WARRIOR Framework** and the transformative potential of living an integrated life.

So, what are you waiting for? Start integrating your life today. Unify your battle plan, unleash the **WARRIOR** within, and create a life that's not just wealthy but truly rich-ass in every way. You got this!

You've explored the power of Integration, learning how to unify your battle plan, prioritize presence, create a values-driven business, and leverage the synergy advantage. Now, delve deeper into the sacrifices required to achieve your dreams. Watch our video "Dreams Come At A Price" at Elliott Training Academy (ETA). Scan the QR code to watch the video and begin integrating your life today.

CHAPTER 18

OWNERSHIP

COMMAND YOUR DESTINY

Look, let's talk about something real—Ownership. This isn't some fluffy self-help concept. This is the bedrock of the **WARRIOR Framework**. It's the key to unlocking your full potential, commanding your destiny, and building a life that most people only dream of. Ownership means taking 100% responsibility for your life—the good, the bad, and the ugly. It means no more excuses, no more blaming others, no more playing the victim. It means stepping up and taking control of your thoughts, actions, and outcomes. This is where true freedom begins. As psychologist Julian Rotter's research on locus of control suggests, taking Ownership is about shifting your belief from being controlled by external forces to believing you have the power to influence events in your life. This internal locus of control is a hallmark of successful individuals.

ZERO EXCUSES: YOUR PATH TO POWER

The victim mentality is a disease. It's a poison that seeps into your soul and keeps you trapped in a cycle of negativity and self-pity. It whispers lies in your ear: "It's not my fault," "I can't help it," "I'm not good enough." These lies become your reality, holding you back from achieving your full potential. But here's the truth: you are not a victim. You are a **WARRIOR**. You have the power to choose your response to any situation. You have the power to create the life you want. But it all starts with eliminating excuses. This aligns with the concept of self-efficacy, as described by psychologist Albert Bandura. Self-efficacy is your belief in your ability to succeed in specific situations. By taking Ownership, you cultivate a stronger sense of self-efficacy, empowering you to overcome challenges and achieve your goals.

Remember Jacqueline's story? She grew up surrounded by gang violence and dysfunction, the first in her family to experience divorce. She could have easily succumbed to the victim mentality, but she didn't. She chose to take Ownership of her life, break free from her past, and build something extraordinary. She said, "I had to break my bloodline, my DNA, and all these generational curses...And I became the woman I needed to be... because of those hardships." Jacqueline didn't let her past define her future. She owned her story and used it as fuel for her growth. That's the power of Ownership. This resonates with the principles of post-traumatic growth (PTG), where individuals who experience trauma often find new meaning and purpose in their lives. Jacqueline's story is a testament to the transformative potential of PTG.

SOLUTION-FOCUSED MINDSET:
TURNING CHALLENGES INTO TRIUMPHS

Problems are inevitable. Life is going to throw you curveballs. The question is, will you dwell on the problem or focus on the solution? A **WARRIOR** doesn't waste time complaining or making excuses. They assess the situation, identify the root cause, and develop a plan of attack. They understand that every challenge is an opportunity for growth, a chance to prove their resilience and emerge stronger. This proactive approach aligns with a growth mindset, as researched by Carol Dweck. Those with a growth mindset embrace challenges as opportunities for learning and development, while those with a fixed mindset view challenges as threats to their self-worth.

THE POWER OF CHOICE: ARCHITECTING YOUR REALITY

Every choice you make, big or small, has consequences. These consequences shape your reality, creating the life you live. Choose wisely. Choose actions that align with your values and propel you toward your goals. Choose to invest in your growth, relationships, and future. Choose to be the **WARRIOR** you were born to be.

Remember the story of the almost-returned coaching program? Even though I'd received value, I was tempted to get his money back. Jacqueline stepped in with a powerful lesson: "Winners get an ROI regardless of the training program." She challenged me to take Ownership of my results and to see myself as a winner, regardless of the circumstances. That single choice to own his potential shaped my trajectory and led us to massive success. This demonstrates the "endowment effect" in action. By valuing the coaching program, even considering its flaws, I showed a sense of Ownership that ultimately led to a greater return on investment.

THE EMPOWERMENT ADVANTAGE: UNLEASHING YOUR INNER WARRIOR

When you take Ownership of your life, you unlock a level of power and control you never thought possible. You become the master of your destiny, the architect of your reality. You develop unshakeable self-confidence, knowing you can overcome any obstacle. You find a deeper sense of purpose, understanding that your choices have meaning and impact.

Think about the Mental Toughness Waiver. It's not just a piece of paper; it's a declaration of Ownership. It's a commitment to pushing yourself beyond your limits, embracing the discomfort of growth, and becoming the best version of yourself. It's a reminder that you are in control of your destiny.

ACTIONABLE STEPS: FROM EXCUSE-MAKER TO OWNER

Ready to take command of your life? Here's a guided exercise to help you identify and eliminate excuses:

- **Identify Your Excuses:** Take out a piece of paper and write down all the excuses you make in your business, relationships, and personal life. Be brutally honest with yourself.

- **Challenge Your Excuses:** For each excuse, ask yourself: "Is this truly valid? Is there anything I could have done differently? What's the real reason I'm not achieving my goal?"

- **Replace Excuses with Solutions:** Brainstorm at least three solutions for each excuse. Focus on what you can control and what actions you can take to move forward.

- **Take Action:** Choose one solution for each excuse and commit to taking action within the next 24 hours. Don't wait for the perfect moment; start now.

MY OWNERSHIP EVOLUTION: A JOURNEY OF TRANSFORMATION

My journey with Ownership has been challenging. I've made my share of mistakes, blamed others, made excuses, and played the victim. But through God's grace and Jacqueline's unwavering support, I've learned to take Ownership of my life. I've learned that true power comes from within, from taking responsibility for my choices and their consequences.

Remember the trash on the road analogy? It's a simple example, but it illustrates a powerful principle: Ownership isn't just about taking responsibility for your actions; it's about taking initiative and positively impacting the world. It's about seeing a problem and being part of the solution.

TESTED BY FIRE: A LESSON IN OWNERSHIP

Life's tough. It throws curveballs, tests your limits, and makes you question everything. The story of Jacqueline's brother's mugging and her getting stung by a scorpion? That's a perfect example of how life can throw you for a loop and how Ownership is the key to getting back on your feet.

Jacqueline's brother was living in Mexico City when he was attacked. It was a bad situation, a random act of violence that nearly cost him his life. He was beaten pretty badly and ended up with a brain aneurysm, a punctured lung, and a whole host of other injuries. He was in rough shape and barely responsive. The news hit us hard. It was a tough time for our family, filled with worry, anger, and uncertainty. The financial strain was immense, too—over half a million dollars in medical expenses, the constant trips to Mexico City, and the emotional weight of seeing him like that. It was a stressful period, a real test of our resilience.

The doctors in Mexico weren't optimistic. They painted a grim picture, telling Jacqueline that her brother likely wouldn't recover. They even suggested unplugging him so they could move him to end his life. Can you imagine the weight of that decision? Most people would crumble under that kind of pressure, but not Jacqueline. She refused to give up. She took Ownership of the situation, demanding a second opinion, researching alternative treatments, and exploring every possible avenue for his recovery. She wasn't about to let a doctor's prognosis dictate her brother's fate. She owned that decision, which fueled her relentless pursuit of a solution.

While Jacqueline was dealing with all of this, juggling the logistics of her brother's care, and pushing back against the doctors' pronouncements, she had a moment... let's just say she had a conversation with the devil. She was frustrated, understandably so. She was questioning everything, wondering why this had happened to her family. But even in that frustration, she found her center. She realized that she had a choice. She could play the victim, or she could take Ownership. She could control her response, even if she couldn't control the situation. She dug in her heels and decided she wouldn't let this break her.

And then, wouldn't you know it, she gets stung by a scorpion while showering. Talk about adding insult to injury! It was a crazy, almost surreal moment. But even then, Jacqueline didn't flinch. She didn't let it derail her. She took Ownership of the situation, treated the sting, and focused on what mattered most—her brother's recovery.

As difficult as it was, that ordeal became a powerful lesson in Ownership. It showed us that real strength isn't about avoiding challenges but how you face them. It's about owning your circumstances, choosing your attitude, and refusing to let setbacks define you. It's about finding the good in the bad, the lesson in the pain, and the opportunity in every obstacle. It's about realizing you always have a choice, even when life throws its worst at you. You choose your response, own your story, and become stronger on the other side. That's the core of the **WARRIOR Framework**—a commitment to Ownership, a refusal to be limited by the past, and a belief in the power to create your future, no matter what. Jacqueline's unwavering belief in her brother, refusal to accept defeat, and willingness to fight for his life, even when the odds were stacked against her, is a testament to the power of Ownership. That's what it means to be a true **WARRIOR**.

THE TRASH ON THE ROAD:
A REFLECTION OF YOUR STANDARDS

Let's talk about standards. Not just talking about them but living them, breathing them, and making them so ingrained in who you are that they become second nature. I want to give you a simple analogy, something you can visualize and apply to every area of your life: the trash on the road.

Picture this: you're walking down the street, nobody around, and you see a piece of trash on the ground. What do you do? Most people would probably keep walking, thinking it's not their problem. "Somebody else will get it," they'd say. But that's not the Bloodline Breaker mentality. That's not Ownership.

The first step is awareness. You see the trash, acknowledge its existence, and take responsibility for the fact that you saw it. That's crucial. Because if you don't own that initial awareness, you can't own the solution. You're giving away your power, surrendering to indifference.

Next, you have to take initiative. One of my core values is taking initiative. I see a problem; I own the solution. So, I see the trash; I pick it up. Simple as that. You might think, "It's just a piece of trash, Andy. What's the big deal?" And that's exactly the point. It's not about the trash itself but the standard it represents.

If I see that trash and don't pick it up, even when nobody's watching, it eats at me. It bothers me for hours. Because it's not just about the physical act of picking up a piece of trash; it's about the internal standard I'm violating. It's about the person I choose to be in that moment. Am I choosing to be someone who takes Ownership, takes pride in their surroundings, and leads by example? Or am I choosing to be someone who looks the other way, passes the buck, accepts mediocrity?

This seemingly small act reflects your standards. It's a microcosm of how you approach life. Do you take Ownership of the little things, the seemingly insignificant details? Because those little things add up. They create a ripple effect, influencing every area of your life, from your business to your relationships to your personal growth.

The higher your standards, the higher the quality of people you'll attract. Weak people who settle for less won't want to be around someone with high standards. It'll make them uncomfortable. They'll feel exposed. But strong people who strive for excellence will gravitate towards you. They'll recognize a kindred spirit who shares their commitment to Ownership and growth.

So, remember what it represents the next time you see a piece of trash on the road. It's not just litter; it's a test, an opportunity to demonstrate your standards, to take Ownership, and to become the kind of leader who inspires others to do the same. It's about building a legacy for yourself, your team, your family, and everyone you impact. This is what it means to be a Bloodline Breaker. It's about owning your shit, even when nobody's watching.

Ownership is not a destination; it's a journey. It's a daily practice, a constant recommitment to taking control of your life. It's about showing up daily as the **WARRIOR** you were born to be—resilient, determined, and unstoppable. So, are you ready to command your destiny? Are you ready to step into your power and create the life you deserve? The choice is yours.

You've explored the power of Ownership, learning how to eliminate excuses, cultivate a solution-focused mindset, harness the power of choice, and unleash your inner WARRIOR. Now, revisit the sacrifices required to achieve your dreams and truly command your destiny. Watch our "Go After Everything" video at Elliott Training Academy (ETA). Scan the QR code to watch the video and continue your journey toward owning your life.

CHAPTER 19

REACH

LEAVE YOUR MARK

Building a life of purpose, passion, and impact isn't just about crushing it in business or stacking up wins. It's about something much bigger, something that transcends your existence. It's about leaving your mark on the world, about making a difference that ripples outwards long after you're gone. This, my friends, is Reach's essence—the **WARRIOR Framework's** final pillar. It's about building a legacy, not just for yourself but for generations to come.

THE WARRIOR'S LEGACY

Think about the great warriors of history whose names echo through time. They weren't just conquerors but builders, innovators, and leaders who left an indelible mark on the world. They understood that true fulfillment comes not from what you take but from what you give, from contributing to something greater than yourself. The Warrior's Legacy is the drive to impact, influence others, and leave a lasting mark. It's about creating a ripple effect, leaving a positive mark not just on the present but also on the future.

It's about tapping into your God-given potential and using it to serve a purpose beyond your ambition. It's about realizing that your time on this earth is limited and making every damn second count.

IMPACT AND INFLUENCE

So, how do you make a difference? How do you create that ripple effect of positive change? It starts with finding a way to give back, to contribute to your community or the world in a way that aligns with your passions and values. It's about asking yourself, "How can I use my gifts and talents to make a difference?" Research has shown that acts of altruism, even small ones, trigger a "helper's high," releasing endorphins and reducing stress. This isn't just feel-good fluff; it's science. Giving back is a win-win, benefiting both the giver and the receiver.

Maybe it's mentoring a young entrepreneur, volunteering at a local charity, or donating to a cause you believe in. It could simply positively influence those around you, showing them what's possible when you live a life of purpose and integrity. The point is, it doesn't have to be some grand, earth-shattering gesture. Even small acts of kindness and service can profoundly impact you, creating a ripple effect beyond your initial action. This is the power of social contagion—positive actions inspire more positive actions, creating a wave of change.

BECOMING A MORAL AUTHORITY

Now, let's talk about moral authority. This isn't about preaching or forcing your beliefs on others. It's about living a life of integrity and purpose so powerfully that it inspires others to raise their standards. It's about becoming the example, the living embodiment of what's possible when you commit to Total Recreation. This ties directly into transformational leadership, where leaders inspire and motivate followers through coercion, example, and shared vision.

When you live with integrity, when your actions align with your words, you earn the respect and trust of those around you. You become a magnet for talent, drawing people who want to be a part of something bigger than themselves. You become a moral authority, a leader who inspires others to step into their greatness.

BUILDING AN ARMY OF WARRIORS

And that, my friends, is how you build an army of warriors. It's not about creating followers but empowering those around you to become leaders. It's about mentoring others, sharing your knowledge, and igniting the fire within them. Studies have consistently shown the profound impact of mentorship programs on the mentees and the mentors themselves, fostering growth, leadership, and a sense of purpose.

Think about it. What's more impactful than achieving success alone or building a team of unstoppable forces changing the world alongside you? True leadership is about empowering others and creating a ripple effect of positive change that extends far beyond your Reach.

THE LEGACY ADVANTAGE

When you reach beyond yourself and focus on making a difference in the lives of others, you unlock something extraordinary—the Legacy Advantage. It's a sense of purpose and connection that transcends your existence, a legacy that outlives you. The concept of legacy is deeply ingrained in human culture, varying in its interpretation across societies yet consistently emphasizing the values, impact, and contributions one makes to the world.

It's about knowing that your impact on the world will continue to ripple outwards long after you're gone, inspiring future generations to rise and achieve their greatness. It's about leaving the world a better place than you found it.

ACTIONABLE STEPS

So, how do you start building your legacy? How do you identify your passions and plan to make a difference? Here is a guided exercise to get you started:

1. **Identify Your Passions:** What are you genuinely passionate about? What gets you fired up and makes you want to jump out of bed in the morning? Write it down.

2. **Identify Your Skills and Talents:** What are you good at? What unique gifts and talents do you have to offer the world? Write it down.

3. **Brainstorm Ways to Make a Difference:** How can you use your passions and talents to contribute to something greater than yourself? Think big, and do not hold back. Write down every idea that comes to mind.

4. **Create an Action Plan:** Choose one or two ideas that resonate most with you and create an action plan. Break down your goals into smaller, manageable steps. What can you do today, this week, and this month to move closer to your vision?

5. **Take Action:** This is the most important step. Don't just talk about it; be about it. Start taking action towards your goals, even if it's just one small step daily. Remember, the compound effect is real. Small, consistent actions over time lead to massive results.

ANDY'S REACH

For me, Reach is about building a movement, about inspiring others to break free from their limitations and live their richest lives. It's about showing people what's possible when you commit to Total Recreation and unleash the warrior within.

I'm investing in myself, my team, and the resources that will allow me to amplify my message and reach more people. I'm building a platform that will empower others to achieve their greatness, creating a ripple effect of positive change that will transform lives and communities for generations to come. I'm building a legacy for myself, my family, my team, and the world. And with God's grace, I'm just getting started.

Here are a few stories that illustrate the power of Reach:

THE DISCOMFORT ZONE EXERCISE

Let's explore this discomfort zone exercise and its connection to Reach. I sometimes do a little exercise to shake things up with my team. I take them to the mall—yeah, the mall—and tell them, "Everybody, we're going to shake a hundred hands. Right now. Let's go."

They look at me like I've sprouted a second head. "what do you mean? Shake a hundred hands? Just…walk up to strangers?"

Damn right. We're going to walk around that mall, and we're going to shake hands with a hundred people. We will smile, make eye contact, and connect with strangers. We're going to get uncomfortable until we're not uncomfortable anymore.

Most people avoid discomfort like the plague. They stick to what they know, what feels safe and familiar. But let me tell you something—growth doesn't happen in your comfort zone. Growth happens when you push past those boundaries, embrace the uncomfortable, and step into the unknown.

This exercise is not just about shaking hands but mastering the art of connection. It's about building confidence, overcoming fear, and becoming the kind of person who can connect with anyone anytime, anywhere.

Think about it. How many opportunities have you missed because you were too afraid to approach someone, start a conversation, or put yourself out there? How many potential clients, mentors, or friends have you let slip through your fingers because you were clinging to your comfort zone?

This exercise is about breaking free from those limitations. It's about building an army of warriors who can connect with strangers, build rapport, and create opportunities out of thin air. It's about becoming a master of influence, a leader who can inspire others to action. And that, my friends, is a powerful tool for achieving Reach. It's about pushing past your limits, embracing the uncomfortable, and becoming someone who can impact the world.

MY PLEDGE TO PATRICK BET-DAVID

I've talked about the power of proximity, about surrounding yourself with greatness. It's a principle I live by. I've invested heavily in mentorship, including spending half a million on training with Patrick Bet-David. It sounds crazy, but let me explain why this second investment with Patrick was crucial.

The first time I trained with Patrick, I learned a ton about strategy, mindset, and business building. But this second round? It was about going deeper and immersing myself further in his world. This wasn't just about adding more tools to my toolbox but a complete transformation.

See Patrick's force of nature. HHe'sbuilt a massive empire and operates on a different level. This time, I wanted to understand what he does and how he does it. I wanted to decode his DNA and understand his mind's inner workings.

I spent time with him, observed him in action, and picked his brain about everything from sales and leadership to building a winning team and creating a lasting legacy. I wanted to absorb his **WARRIOR** energy, to integrate his relentless drive and unwavering belief into my being.

This investment was not just about learning new information but a fundamental shift in my identity. It was about pushing past my perceived limitations and stepping into a new level of greatness. It was about expanding my vision and seeing what's possible when you commit to Reach.

And let me tell you, the return on that investment has been immeasurable. It's notIIt'snot just about the financial gains, although those have been significant. It's about the clarity, confidence, and unshakable belief in myself that I gained from this deeper level of mentorship. It's about becoming the kind of person who can achieve anything they set their mind to and make a real impact on the world. It's About Reach. And that, my friends, is priceless.

This whole Patrick Bet-David story isn't just about me learning from him. It's about something much bigger: a shared vision, a common purpose, and a commitment to building something extraordinary.

See, Patrick and I are cut from the same cloth. We both believe in hard work, the relentless pursuit of excellence, and the power of building a tribe of warriors. We both are passionate about empowering others, breaking bloodlines, and leaving a lasting legacy.

That's why I pledged Patrick. I told him, "Brother, I'm not just here to learn from you. I'm here to join forces with you. I am here to help you build an army of **WARRIORS** who will change the world." We're talking about a movement, a force for good that will disrupt the status quo and empower millions to achieve their full potential. We're discussing creating a legacy that will ripple outwards for generations.

This isn't just about business; it's about impact. It's about leaving the world a better place than we found it and creating a brighter future for our kids and generations.

With God as our witness, we're just getting started. So buckle up because this ride will get wild. We're rebuilding, changing the world, and not stopping until we reach the top.

These stories are just a glimpse into the power of Reach. They show that true fulfillment comes from contributing to something greater than yourself, leaving your mark on the world, and building a legacy that outlives you. So, what's your story going to be? What kind of impact are you going to make on the world? The choice is yours. Now, go out there and make it happen.

You've explored the power of Reach, learning how to build a Warrior's legacy, maximize impact and influence, become a moral authority, and build an army of WARRIORS. Now, let's shift gears and focus on a crucial element of maintaining your Reach: preventing complacency. Watch our video "How To Prevent Getting Comfortable" at Elliott Training Academy (ETA). Scan the QR code to watch the video and continue your journey toward leaving your mark on the world.

CHAPTER 20

THE WARRIOR'S CODE

YOUR PATH TO TOTAL RECREATION

Brothers and sisters, warriors in the making, we've journeyed together through the trenches of transformation, exploring the mind, body, and spirit battlefields. We've dissected the **WARRIOR Framework**, pillar by pillar, uncovering the secrets to unlocking your full potential and creating a life of purpose, passion, and unwavering faith. Now, it's time to forge your path, create your **WARRIOR'S** Code, and embark on the journey of a lifetime.

THE WARRIOR'S PATH: A ROADMAP TO TOTAL RECREATION

Let's recap the core principles that form the foundation of the **WARRIOR Framework**, the seven pillars that will guide you on your quest for Total Recreation:

 WORKOUT
Activate your body and mind for war. This isn't just about physical fitness; it's about building a foundation of strength, resilience, and unwavering

energy that fuels every aspect of your life. It's about pushing your limits, embracing the suck, and forging an unbreakable spirit.

AWARENESS
Know your battlefield. This is about developing the Warrior's Eye, that laser-sharp focus that allows you to see yourself, your surroundings, and the challenges in your path. It's about asking the tough questions, seeking feedback, and unmasking the limiting beliefs that hold you back.

RELATIONSHIPS
Build your unrecruitable tribe. This is about surrounding yourself with a loyal band of brothers and sisters who will support you, challenge you, and celebrate your victories like their own. It's about creating a network of trust, loyalty, and shared purpose to empower you to achieve greatness.

RECREATE
Forge your new armor. This is about constantly shedding the old you—the limitations, fears, doubts—and embracing the new, more powerful version of yourself. It's about evolving, adapting, and becoming even more badass than you were yesterday.

INTEGRATION
Unify your battle plan. This isn't about balance; it's about integration. It's about weaving together the different strands of your life—your mind, body, spirit, family, and business—into a seamless tapestry of purpose and fulfillment.

OWNERSHIP
Command your destiny. This is about taking 100% responsibility for your life—the good, the bad, and the ugly. It's about eliminating excuses, focusing on solutions, and becoming the master of your fate.

REACH
Leave your mark. This is about making a difference in the world, about leaving a legacy that ripples outwards long after you're gone. It's about using your gifts and talents to serve others, inspire change, and build a brighter future for future generations.

CREATING YOUR CODE:
A WARRIOR'S MANIFESTO

Now, it's time to create your personal **WARRIOR'S** Code, a manifesto for living that will guide your actions, shape your decisions, and empower you to create the life you deserve. This is more than just setting goals; it's about defining your values, clarifying your purpose, and committing to living a life of strength, integrity, and impact.

Here's a guided exercise to help you forge your own **WARRIOR'S** Code:

- **Define Your Values:** What principles are non-negotiable for you? What do you stand for? What kind of person do you want to be? Write down your top five core values.

- **Set Your Goals:** What do you want to achieve in your business, relationships, personal growth, and impact on the world? Be specific, measurable, achievable, relevant, and time-bound (SMART). Write down your top three goals for each area.

- **Craft Your Code:** Based on your values and goals, create a set of principles that will guide your actions and decisions. These should be short, powerful statements reflecting your commitment to living the **WARRIOR** way. For example: "I will prioritize my health and well-being," "I will cultivate strong relationships," "I will take radical ownership of my life," and "I will use my success to make a difference in the world."

- **Live Your Code:** This is the most important step. Post your **WARRIOR'S** Code somewhere you'll see it every day—on your bathroom mirror, your desk, or even your phone's lock screen. Review it regularly, and make sure your actions align with your principles. You can see our company values everywhere. That's our **WARRIOR'S** code for business.

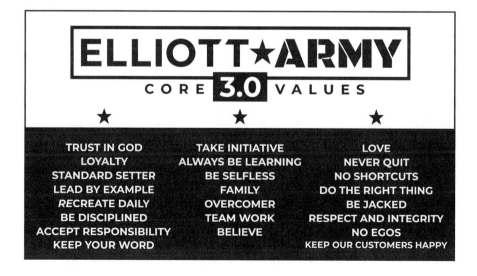

ELLIOTT★ARMY
CORE 3.0 VALUES

★　　　★　　　★

TRUST IN GOD	TAKE INITIATIVE	LOVE
LOYALTY	ALWAYS BE LEARNING	NEVER QUIT
STANDARD SETTER	BE SELFLESS	NO SHORTCUTS
LEAD BY EXAMPLE	FAMILY	DO THE RIGHT THING
*RE*CREATE DAILY	OVERCOMER	BE JACKED
BE DISCIPLINED	TEAM WORK	RESPECT AND INTEGRITY
ACCEPT RESPONSIBILITY	BELIEVE	NO EGOS
KEEP YOUR WORD		KEEP OUR CUSTOMERS HAPPY

THE JOURNEY OF A LIFETIME: EMBRACE THE GRIND

The **WARRIOR'S** path is not a destination but a lifelong journey of growth, transformation, and service. There will be challenges, setbacks, and moments when you want to quit. But that's where the real growth happens, where you forge your strength, resilience, and unwavering faith.

Embrace the grind, warriors. Embrace the discomfort, the challenges, and the lessons that life throws your way because it's in those moments, in the crucible of adversity, that you discover your true potential and become the **WARRIOR** you were born to be.

A CALL TO ARMS: UNLEASH THE WARRIOR WITHIN

The world needs your light, unique gifts, and unwavering spirit. It's time to step up, take Ownership of your destiny, and create a life that is both successful and meaningful. It's time to unleash the **WARRIOR** within and conquer your damn life.

ANDY'S WARRIOR CODE

My Code, forged in the fires of experience setbacks and fueled by an unwavering faith in God and myself, is more than just words on a page. It's the bedrock of my existence, the compass guiding my every action, and the legacy I strive to leave behind. This is my **WARRIOR** Code:

- Workout: The Foundation of the **WARRIOR**

  - **The 4% Commitment:** One hour a day. No excuses. This isn't about vanity but building a temple of strength, resilience, and unwavering energy. It's about fueling the Ferrari treating my body like the high-performance machine it is. (Chapter 13)

  - **The Do Not Disturb Zone:** When I train, I go dark. No distractions. This is about building mental toughness and forging an unbreakable focus that carries over into every aspect of my life. (Chapter 13)

- **3 Cars, 200 Calls, 3 Miles:** My non-negotiables. The daily grind that built my discipline, resilience, and unwavering commitment. The pain of the run was fuel for the fire, a constant reminder that mediocrity is not an option. (Chapter 13)

- **The 5 AM Club & The Cold Plunge:** My daily ritual of self-improvement, a shock to the system that ignites my **WARRIOR** spirit and sets the tone for a day of conquest. A little friendly competition with Jacqueline never hurts, either. (Chapter 13)

- **Awareness: Know Your Battlefield**

  - **The Warrior's Eye:** I ask the tough questions, confront my demons head-on, and seek the uncomfortable truths that set me free. I'm brutally honest with myself and open to feedback, even when it stings. (Chapter 14)

  - **Running on Empty:** The humbling reminder that even **WARRIORS** can slip up. It's a lesson in staying present, checking the fuel gauge of my life, and never taking anything for granted. (Chapter 14)

  - **The Power of Proximity:** I invest in myself, surround myself with greatness (like my half-million dollar investment with Patrick Bet-David), and soak up the wisdom of those who have walked the path before me. (Chapter 14)

- **Relationships: My Unrecruitable Tribe**

  - **"I'm Not Your Babysitter":** I empower my team, challenge them to grow, and create heroes, not followers. I invest in their lives, not just their production. I trust them, but they earn it. (Chapter 15)

  - **Building Unbreakable Bonds:** My clients aren't just transactions but part of my tribe. I care about their success, their well-being, their lives. I shower them with love, certainty, and unwavering support. (Chapter 15)

- **Recreate: Forge Your New Armor**

  - **The Eagle Rebirth:** I shed the old feathers of doubt and fear, embrace the painful process of molting, and emerge stronger, more resilient, and ready to conquer anything. (Chapter 16)

  - **"Winners Get an ROI":** Jacqueline's wisdom is a constant reminder that my success is my responsibility, regardless of the circumstances. I extract value from every investment, every experience, every challenge. (Chapter 16)

- Integration: Unify Your Battle Plan

  - **The $100,000 Car Sacrifice:** We bet on our vision, not material possessions. We downsized, sacrificed comfort, and built our war room, a testament to our shared commitment and unwavering faith. (Chapter 17)

  - **Jacqueline at 3:30 AM:** The image of unwavering dedication, a reminder that building a legacy takes sacrifice, relentless pursuit of growth, and a partner in the trenches with you. (Chapter 17)

- Ownership: Command Your Destiny

  - **Zero Excuses:** I own my shit. The good, the bad, and the ugly. I choose my response, control my actions, and command my destiny. (Chapter 18)

  - **Tested by Fire:** Jacqueline's unwavering belief in her brother and her refusal to accept defeat, even in the face of unimaginable challenges, is a constant source of inspiration. I choose Ownership, even when life throws its worst. (Chapter 18)

  - **The Trash on the Road:** My daily reminder that Ownership is about standards, taking initiative, and leading by example, even when no one's watching. (Chapter 18)

- Reach: Leave Your Mark

  - **The Discomfort Zone Exercise:** I push my team (and myself) beyond our limits, embracing the uncomfortable to master the art of connection and unlock the power of influence. (Chapter 19)

  - **My Pledge to Patrick Bet-David:** I invest in my growth, not just for myself, but to build an army of **WARRIORS** who will change the world. It's about a shared vision, a common purpose, and a commitment to leaving a legacy. (Chapter 19)

THE WARRIOR'S TRIFECTA: PHYSICAL, MENTAL, BUSINESS

You can't be great in business if you're not in the right mindset, and you can't get in the right mindset if you're not in great physical shape. It's a synergistic cycle, a feedback loop of excellence that fuels my journey.

Now, warriors, it's your turn. You've been equipped with the WARRIOR Framework, a battle-tested blueprint for Total Recreation. You've seen how each pillar—Workout, Awareness, Relationships, Recreate, Integration, Ownership, and Reach—interlocks to create a life of purpose, passion, and unwavering faith. You've witnessed the power of these principles in my own life, in Jacqueline's journey, and in the stories of countless others who have embraced the WARRIOR's path. But knowledge without action is just potential. It's time to take what you've learned, forge your own WARRIOR's Code, and step into the arena of life, ready to conquer your challenges and create the legacy you were born to leave. Don't go it alone. My team and I are here to support you every step of the way. Schedule your FREE coaching call with my team today, and let us help you unleash the WARRIOR within and embark on the journey of a lifetime. Scan the QR code to watch a short video from me and take the first step towards Total Recreation.